The Dimensions of Ethics

The Dimensions of Ethics
An Introduction to Ethical Theory

Wilfrid J. Waluchow

broadview press

National Library of Canada Cataloguing in Publication

Waluchow, Wilfrid J., 1953–
    The dimensions of ethics : an introduction to ethical theory / Wilfrid J. Waluchow.

Includes bibliographical references and index.
ISBN 1-55111-450-X

    1. Ethics--Textbooks. I. Title.

BJ1012.W34 2003   170   C2003-900862-2

Broadview Press, Ltd. is an independent, international publishing house, incorporated in 1985. Broadview believes in shared ownership, both with its employees and with the general public; since the year 2000 Broadview shares have traded publicly on the Toronto Venture Exchange under the symbol BDP.

We welcome any comments and suggestions regarding any aspect of our publications—please feel free to contact us at the addresses below, or at broadview@broadviewpress.com / customerservice@broadviewpress.com

North America
Post Office Box 1243,
Peterborough, Ontario,
Canada K9J 7H5
Tel: (705) 743-8990
Fax: (705) 743-8353

3576 California Road,
Orchard Park, New York
USA 14127

UK, Ireland, and
Continental Europe
Plymbridge
Distributors, Ltd.
Estover Road
Plymouth PL6 7PY
UK
Tel: (01752) 202301
Fax: (01752) 202333
orders@plymbridge.com

Australia and
New Zealand
UNIREPS
University of
New South Wales
Sydney, NSW, 2052
Tel: + 61 2 96640999
Fax: + 61 2 96645420
info.press@unsw.edu.au

www.broadviewpress.com

Broadview Press Ltd. gratefully acknowledges the financial support of the Government of Canada through the Book Publishing Industry Development Program for our publishing activities.

Typeset by Zack Taylor, www.zacktaylor.com.

Printed in Canada

For Donna, who continues to make it all worthwhile

Contents

Contents

Acknowledgements

A number of individuals have contributed in various ways to the writing of this book. I wish to begin by acknowledging the contribution of my late friend and colleague, John E. Thomas, who helped me write an introductory essay for our book, *Well and Good*, from which the current work springs. I also owe a debt of gratitude to several anonymous reviewers for Broadview Press and to Matthew Barber whose help in drafting Chapter Five was immensely valuable. Finally, I wish to thank the Broadview editorial staff whose kindness, courtesy, and professionalism never cease to amaze me.

Part I
Meta-ethics

One
The Many Dimensions
of Ethical Theory

Ethical Theory

The topic of this book is ethical theory. But what is an ethical theory? How, if at all, do ethical theory and morality differ? These seemingly simple questions admit of no easy answer. Sometimes, it seems, the terms "ethics" and "morality," and cognate terms like "ethical" and "moral" are treated as equivalent in meaning. When Kim says, "His ethics are questionable" she may well mean much the same thing by the term "ethics" as Mike means by "morality" when he replies, "His moral beliefs are perfectly fine; in fact, he's quite the moral person." Yet one often encounters claims like the following: "I am worried about the ethical and moral dimensions of stem cell research." Unless speakers who talk this way are guilty of simple redundancy in employing both "ethical" and "moral" in this way, there must be some difference in meaning intended or presupposed. But what could that difference be?

Sometimes, people seem to distinguish the moral and the ethical by suggesting that ethics concern profound questions of considerable consequence, for example, abortion or the death penalty. Morality, on the other hand, is thought to involve relatively trivial matters like sexual mores, or the consumption of harmless but illegal drugs like marijuana. In such cases we talk of the legal enforcement of morality, and many question whether coercive prevention of such relatively trivial and harmless conduct is a good idea. On the other hand, some use these terms to make a distinction which goes exactly the other way. Moral questions are thought to be the profound ones, while questions of ethics find their place lower on the scale of relative importance. When Kristi asks "Is it ethical for Bob to encourage his clients to move with him when he joins another firm," her judgment might be based on Bob's having transgressed a professional code of business ethics, a code which would not suitably be described as a code of morality. When, on the other hand, Kristi condemns the death penalty, she might think that the force of her condemnation is not adequately captured were she to say that the practice is (merely) unethical. She might insist on condemning it as profoundly immoral, thus capturing the depth of her condemnation.

So what do we say about all this? Can we safely draw a distinction between the **ethical** and the **moral**? Faced with these different usages, we propose in this book to take the first route suggested by the discussion between Mike and Kim. "Ethics" and "morality" and all other cognate terms such as "ethical" and "moral" will, for the most part, be treated as equivalent in meaning. We will, however, draw an important distinction between ethical theory, on the one hand, and morality (or ethics), on the other.

Ethical theory, as we will understand it here, is a branch of philosophy. It is an attempt to understand, interpret and to some extent guide, the practice of morality. It is

moral philosophy: that is, philosophical thinking about, or analysis of, moral problems, dilemmas, and concepts, and the making of moral judgments. It seeks to impart understanding and clarity to a practice with which we are all, in one way or another, thoroughly familiar. But familiarity is not always accompanied by clarity and understanding. We can all tell time and think we know what time is. But as Augustine famously said, "What then is time? If no one asks me I know: if I wish to explain it to one that asks, I know not."[1] The same is true of morality. We all have some more or less intuitive understanding of what morality is about, but if asked to explain its nature, or the concepts in terms of which we make moral judgments, most people would be hard pressed to come up with satisfactory answers. In the case of the concept of time this lack of understanding may not much matter. But the same cannot be said of morality. Our moral judgments are often of the utmost importance. What can be of greater consequence than deciding whether, when, and why it is morally right or permissible to withdraw life support from a cherished loved one? What can be more important than deciding whether it is morally permissible to shoot down a hijacked aircraft containing many innocent people in order to save a greater number of lives? Or if one finds these examples a bit too dramatic and atypical, what can be more important than deciding whether, when and why it is permissible to break a promise to one's children, or to give money to charity: money that might otherwise be spent on buying better clothes for the kids? Different understandings of morality and its philosophical underpinnings can sometimes yield different moral judgments. So we all need moral philosophy. We need the clarity of thought and, it is hoped, integrity of action that it can provide. If moral philosophy cannot, in the end, tell us what to do, it can at the very least tell us what we mean when we claim to have done the morally right thing. It can also tell us what the fundamental bases of such moral claims might be, and disclose to us various constellations of moral rules, principles, values, and approaches that might be used in making moral judgments. These are the tasks of the moral philosopher and her ethical theories and it should now be clear that they are of utmost importance. Let us begin with some preliminary philosophical thoughts on the nature of morality and on how moral judgments differ from a myriad of other kinds of judgments we often make. This will provide us with a good entry point into the fascinating world of moral philosophy.

The Moral

Most of us are usually able to detect moral judgments when we see them. When Ted says: "Driving with a blood alcohol level of .09 is **wrong** because it violates the traffic code of Saskatchewan," he does not make a moral judgment, he makes a **legal** one. He appeals, not to a moral principle or rule as a standard against which to measure his actions but to a legal rule found in the Saskatchewan traffic code. When, on the other hand, Stella asks: "Yes, but do we always have an obligation to obey this law? After all, most people are still perfectly sober when they register .09, so what's the harm?" she is making a **moral** judgment. She is questioning whether we have a moral obligation to obey the laws of Saskatchewan on each and every occasion, and appealing to a law will not help her in answering this particular question.

So most of us can usually tell the difference between a legal judgment and a moral one. When Spiro says "This strawberry ice cream is really **good**" he too expresses something other than a moral judgment. In this instance, he expresses what we might call a simple judgment of **taste**. But when Laurie replies "Yes, but don't you think we **owe** it to the kids to get them some too?" she expresses a moral judgment, based on either the principle requiring parents to be benevolent towards their children, or one requiring us to keep our promises.

Suppose now that Barry offers the following assessment of the latest Tom Clancy novel: "The plot is pretty good, but the character development is dreadfully thin. So, overall, I think the book is pretty bad." Barry is clearly not making a moral judgment. But neither is he making a legal judgment or uttering a simple judgment of taste. Rather, he expresses what philosophers call an **aesthetic judgment**, one based on the merit of Clancy's novel as a work of literature or art. This is a judgment which makes reference, not to moral value, but to "aesthetic value." When Mark replies: "All of this is irrelevant. There is no way that someone should be publishing a book about terrorist attacks on public buildings right after the destruction of the World Trade Center, the assault on the Pentagon, and the cold blooded murder of thousands of innocent people" he makes a moral judgment. He is not commenting on the artistic value of Clancy's book, but on the moral propriety of publishing it immediately after the events of September 11, 2001. Whether the book has aesthetic value is not at issue for Mark.

Finally, suppose that Scott says to Ann, "I need to play more golf. It's good for my sense of well being." Scott is making what philosophers call a **prudential** judgment, one based solely on the interests of the individual whose conduct or character are in question. It is a judgment about what it is rational for him to do in order to promote his own welfare or well being. When Ann replies: "But you owe it to the kids to spend more time with them. And to top it off you promised them you would," she makes a moral judgment. She appeals, not only to what is in Scott's best interests, but also to the interests of the others who are affected by his conduct. Of course Ann also appeals to the prior commitment that Scott made to the children. This is a commitment based on a practice central to moral life, namely, the practice of promising. Prudential judgments concern, then, the interests of individual actors. The interests of others are relevant only to the extent that they impact on the individual actor's own interests. It is usually taken to be a mark of the moral that the interests of other people count too.

So we all have some idea of a moral judgment when we see one. And most of us have a more or less intuitive, or common sense, idea of some of the basic features of morality, the phenomenon which ethical theory seeks to understand, explain and perhaps guide. Moral judgments appeal to **standards** of some kind against which actions, motives, traits of character and so on are measured and assessed. In this respect they are unlike simple judgments of taste, where appeal to standards is often unnecessary, or perhaps even out of place. Were Spiro asked why he finds the strawberry ice cream particularly good, it would be perfectly appropriate for him to reply: "No reason, it just strikes me that way." Such a reply would not be appropriate were Laurie asked to explain why they owe it to the kids to bring home some ice cream. In the case of moral judgments it is always appropriate to ask for a **reason** which **justifies** or **warrants** the judgment made. In many instances this reason will lie in a rule or principle of some kind. But where do we find such rules and principles? And do they require their own justification or warrant? Among the reasons why Spiro and Laurie ought to bring home some ice cream is that they promised to do so. And the reason they ought to keep that promise is the general moral principle that, barring highly unusual circumstances, we always ought to keep our promises. But what justifies or warrants this particular principle? What reason could be given for it?

In the view of most philosophers we cannot just look up moral principles in something analogous to the Saskatchewan traffic code, though there are exceptions. **Divine Command** theories of morality posit, in effect, a "moral code" decreed by God which is roughly analogous to the traffic code of Saskatchewan. Just as Stella can discern her legal obligation by looking to the rules decreed by the Saskatchewan legislature, the Divine Command theorist claims that we can discover our moral obligations by looking to the moral code decreed by God in, e.g., the Bible or the Koran. Another possible exception can be found in theories which stress the importance of **professional codes of ethics**, such as the codes of the Canadian and American Medical Associations, which attempt to specify the ethical obligations of health care workers. On such theories moral and legal justification are closely analogous to one another. A third possible exception lies in forms of **moral relativism** which assert that moral principles and rules consist of a set of fundamental conventions and practices accepted within a given society or community. We cannot, of course, just look up a society's conventions in an authoritative text, as we can its traffic laws or its professional codes. But it is still possible, at least in theory, to **discover** our moral obligations by way of **empirical** observation. We can discover our obligations by determining which conventions happen to be part of our society's conventional moral practices, and we can fulfil our moral responsibilities by making sure that our actions conform with these conventions. In reality, of course, things are not always so straightforward. Conventional rules, no less than the commands of God or the rules found in codes of ethics, must be interpreted in the light of new circumstances. But, as we shall see in later chapters, this cannot usually be done except by addressing, for oneself, the moral questions raised by the new circumstances.

These exceptions aside, most philosophers believe that moral principles and rules are not empirically discoverable in codes or sets of conventional rules. And few believe that moral judgments require no justification at all, though (as we shall see later) there are crude forms of a theory called **Emotivism** according to which moral judgments are indeed analogous to Spiro's views about strawberry ice cream. But if moral judgments must be justified, and if the rules and principles used to justify them are not subject to empirical discovery, how **do** we go about justifying our moral claims? There is, unfortunately, no easy or straightforward answer to this question, and we will not pretend otherwise. Theorists differ not only in their moral judgments, and about the rules and principles which justify them, they also differ in their philosophical views about the nature of moral argumentation. Some hold that we have a special kind of **moral intuition** which allows us to discern the truth of basic moral principles. According to the medieval natural law philosopher, St. Thomas Aquinas, for example, the moral principle that one ought to kill no human person is as evident to the human mind as the basic principles of reasoning, such as the law of non-contradiction that nothing can be both F and not-F, at the same time, in the same place and in the same respect. Most contemporary philosophers, however, reject the claim that moral standards are just self-evident to any rational person. But if we follow their lead, it is not at all clear how one is to go about justifying one's belief in certain moral standards. Modern social contract theorists, attempt to solve the issue of moral justification by claiming that moral principles are those that would be agreed upon by a group of fully rational, prudentially motivated individuals concerned to extricate themselves from what Thomas Hobbes called "the state of nature" where life is "solitary, poor, nasty, brutish and short."[2] Morality, on this view, is a kind of contractual commitment agreed upon by people concerned to promote their mutual self interest. And so moral judgments are, in the end, derivable from simpler judgments of prudence. Many contemporary philosophers find the social contract theory of morality objectionable on a number of grounds, which we will explore later. But if we reject both moral intuition and the social contract theory, it is not obvious how we should go about justifying our moral judgments.

This book makes no attempt to argue in favour of particular answers to these methodological questions posed in ethical theory. Nor will we declare allegiance to any particular substantive theory of basic moral commitments. Instead, we will explore, with a critical eye, a wide range of answers offered by philosophers throughout the history of western thought and different accounts of the status of moral principles, rules and values.[3] We will also examine, in some detail, a variety of theories purporting to outline the basic standards underlying our moral judgments. As we shall see, some theories, such as John Stuart Mill's **Act Utilitarianism**, posit one fundamental principle from which all other subordinate principles and rules can be derived. Others, such as W.D. Ross's **mixed deontological theory**, claim that there are a number of fundamental moral principles none of which is more basic than the others. But, as noted above, exactly how one goes about choosing between Ross and Mill, or the myriad other ethical theories proposed over the centuries, is by no means easy to determine. The same can be said about theories concerning the ultimate objects of moral **value**. Mill posits one fundamental object of value — happiness — in terms of which all of our moral judgments are ultimately to be explained and justified. But others, e.g., G.E. Moore and modern proponents of **Preference Utilitarianism**, are unwilling to reduce moral value to a single object or quality. According to Moore there are a number of objects of moral value (e.g., friendship and aesthetic experience) and these are valuable independently of whether they contribute to human happiness. According to preference utilitarians what is ultimately of value in life depends on the rational preferences people happen to have. One person's ultimate preference might be for happiness, but someone else's ultimate preference might be for the creation of great art, even at the expense of human happiness.

It is a fact of moral life that reasonable and conscientious individuals both can and do, at the end of the day, disagree in their moral judgments, and about how, if at all, these are to be justified. It would be far simpler were there one ethical theory providing a uniquely correct set of standards to apply in making moral evaluations. The only problems then remaining would be problems of **casuistry** — that is problems concerning the application of rules or principles to particular factual circumstances. Suppose that the correct moral principle requires that we always do whatever will lead, in the particular circumstances in question, to the greatest happiness of the greatest number. Were this the correct foundational moral principle, then all we would have to do to determine our moral obligations would be to tote up the degrees of happiness and unhappiness caused by the various courses of action open to us, and take the appropriate action. If shooting down a hijacked airliner containing many innocent passengers would result in the saving of a far greater number of innocent lives on the ground, then that would be the right thing to do. Application of the correct moral principle would determine this course of action as the right one to pursue. This would remove the need to agonize over whether it is wrong **intentionally** to cause by one's own hand the death of innocent people, even when one **foresees** that failure to do so will result in the deaths, by someone else's hand, of a far greater number of innocent people. Moral philosophy, however, has yet to provide a uniquely correct set of standards which would effectively remove all such doubts. The fact remains that moral thinking, at least at this stage in our development as moral creatures, requires more than mere casuistry, more than the simple application of an agreed set of standards to different factual situations.

All this is not to say, however, that the choice among different theories and approaches is entirely arbitrary, or that we have not, over the many centuries of moral thinking, been able to make progress. As we gain further understanding of ourselves and the world around us, we should expect both our ethical theories and our moral practices to improve. Slavery, for example, was once considered morally acceptable by the peoples of many western countries, such as France, Great Britain, and the United States. The practice is now almost universally condemned as the moral abomination that it surely is. The same can be said about ethical theory. Although it has been questioned whether philosophers have truly progressed beyond the theories of Plato and Aristotle, few would deny that **some** progress has occurred over the centuries.[4] At one time many people thought that naturally occurring phenomena provided the answers to moral questions. Few, if any, moral agents would now accept a theory which included floods and locusts as reliable indicators of our moral responsibilities. In this respect, ethical theory is similar to the sciences, where change and progress are routinely accepted as inevitable and as not threatening the very soundness of the enterprise. Quantum physics is perhaps as fraught with theoretical difficulties as ethical theory, but it would be silly to give up on it because of this fact. And just as there is much to be learned from the history of scientific theory, there are valuable lessons to be learned from the ways in which some of the greatest thinkers within our cultural history have seriously and systematically approached moral questions and the questions of ethical theory. These are thinkers whose theories provide valuable frameworks for moral thinking, frameworks in which current moral disputes are often argued. One cannot get too far in contemporary moral debate without encountering some appeal to the concept of "utility" or the value of "individual autonomy." These concepts are the cornerstones of two of the theories explored in Part II: Mill's act utilitarianism and Kant's deontological ethics.

So perhaps the best we can do at this point in our development as moral creatures is to engage the pursuit of defensible moral beliefs and defensible ethical theories, and to learn as much as we can from those who have tried to do so in the past. In pursuing this important enterprise ourselves we would do well to heed the advice of Mill, who, in his classic political treatise, *On Liberty*, observed that "conflicting doctrines, instead of one being true and the other false, [often] share the truth between them, and the non-conforming opinion is needed to supply the remainder of the truth of which the received doctrine embodies only a part."[5] We should, in other words, be flexible and leave open the distinct possibility that some measure of truth can be found in virtually all of the ethical theories to be explored below. We might also heed the wise counsel of Aristotle who observed that "precision is not to be sought alike in all discussions. We must be content, in speaking of such subjects [as ethical and political theory], to indicate the truth roughly and in outline."[6]

The Dimensions of Ethical Theory

At the very outset we noted a number of questions which, in one way or another, had to do with morality and ethics. We asked: What is an ethical theory? And how, if at all, do ethical theory and morality differ from one another? An ethical theory, as this phrase is to be understood here, is a **philosophical** theory which seeks to **understand, explain**, and perhaps **guide** us in the practice of making moral judgments.[7] An ethical theory does not report or describe moral beliefs of particular cultures, groups or individuals. It is not identical with what we might call **descriptive ethics**. The historical and sociological inquiries of descriptive ethics can of course be of their own intrinsic interest. They can also be extremely helpful to the moral philosopher, if only because they sometimes reveal the multiplicity of moral perspectives it is possible to take and the options which other reasonable people of good will and integrity have thought morally worthy of pursuit. But the **philosopher** engaged in ethical theory is not out merely to describe moral beliefs and practices. Rather, she wants to say something about the following:

    A. The very nature or status of morality: Is morality a set of rules and principles like the rules found in the Saskatchewan Traffic Code, except that they are decreed by God and not the Saskatchewan legislature? Or is it perhaps a set of rules and principles emerging from a hypothetical "social contract" among human beings concerned to further their mutual self interest? If neither of these alternatives explains what morality is, just what is the answer?

B. The nature and meaning of moral judgments: Do moral judgments merely express our emotions, or our favourable or non-favourable attitudes towards various courses of conduct? If so, does this mean that moral judgments are incapable of being assessed as either true or false? Or do they instead express propositions which are as capable of truth or falsity as any other statements of fact, like the proposition that China has the largest population in the world, or that it is against the custom of Christian men to wear hats while attending church services?

C. The fundamental rules, principles and values justifying moral judgments: Is human happiness the only thing of ultimate value, as Mill thought, or are there other things of ultimate value, perhaps a healthy environment or friendship? In pursuing the moral life, should we aim to ensure that our actions conform to a fundamental principle like the principle of utility or Kant's categorical imperative? Or should our aim perhaps be to foster caring relationships with others, as some feminists urge, or to lead a life of virtue, as the ancient Greek philosopher, Aristotle, advised?

D. More particular moral practices and beliefs: If it is accepted practice in the country in which one is doing business to accept under-the-table payments, is it morally permissible to offer such payments too, even though they are roundly condemned as immoral in all the codes of ethical business practice found within one's own country? Should medical scientists be allowed to create human embryos for the express purpose of extracting stem cells which are then used to grow replacement organs? Is this permissible given that the process of extraction necessarily results in the destruction of the embryo?

A-D represent a range of issues addressed by ethical theory. In addressing A and B, philosophers engage in what is usually called **meta-ethics**. Meta-ethics does not try to answer the general or particular questions posed in C and D. Rather it offers answers to **epistemological** and **metaphysical** questions, and to questions of **meaning**. It tries to answer general philosophical questions like "What does it **mean** to ask whether stem cell research is morally permissible?" or "What kind of **grounds** or **evidence** should one give in support of an answer to this question?" Should one attempt to extract, from an "authoritative" source like the Bible, evidence of God's will on the subject? Or is possible that such appeals to authority are never warranted in moral inquiry, that each of us must always appeal ultimately to our own conscience and attempt to discover our own answer to such a question?

In addressing the questions posed in C and D, we move from meta-ethics and on to **normative ethics**. C concerns what is usually called **general normative ethics**, that is the development of very general schemes of moral principles and/or values in terms of which our more particular moral judgments can be evaluated. Mill's utilitarianism, Aristotle's virtue ethics, and Kant's deontological theory of the categorical imperative, are all examples of general normative ethical theories. D, on the other hand, involves what is usually termed **applied** or **practical ethics**. It is often said that the general ethical theories of Kant, Mill, et al. are of little help in grappling with the complex issues facing us in every day life, including moral issues which arise within the practice of the various professions like law, engineering, medicine and business. It is one thing to be told that one should promote the greatest happiness of the greatest number. It is quite another to determine exactly what this principle requires when faced with doing business in a country whose accepted business practices are condemned by one's profession, or when one is grappling with the question whether to withdraw life support from a young patient in a persistent vegetative state. Applied or practical ethics attempts to deal with these more concrete applications. It is less concerned with justifying the very general and abstract principles endorsed by the likes of Mill, Kant and Aristotle, than with providing reasoned answers to the concrete moral questions of every-day life. Does this mean, then, that the general ethical theories of Kant and Mill are of no interest or value whatsoever? Not at all. Even if Mill, Kant, et al. themselves provide less than complete guidance in answering concrete moral questions, the fact remains that they do provide extremely useful frameworks in terms of which we can grapple with these questions in all their complexity. Mill highlights the important role played by the **consequences** of our actions in discerning the requirements of the moral life. Kant, for his part, points us to the equally important role of **intention**, and to the fact that sometimes the morally right action may **not** bring about the best consequences. It may, in the end, be morally wrong intentionally to bring about the death of those airline passengers even if in so doing we could prevent an even greater loss of human life. Looking at Mill and Kant may help us to determine whether this is indeed the case, or at the very least help us to sort out our own thinking and commitments. Looking at Aristotle might, on the other hand, direct us in an entirely different direction. It may well be, as Aristotle said, that, at the end of the day, the correct question is not "What should I do?" but "What kind of person should I be?" Looking at our moral lives in this light might well give us an insight that is lacking if we restrict ourselves to questions about the rightness or wrongness of particular actions. In framing these important considerations, and fostering philosophical understanding of their role in moral thinking, the general normative theories of philosophers like Aristotle, Mill and Kant can play a pivotal role in helping us to think and act morally. They can help us to deal with the otherwise perplexing array of factors at play when we attempt to make moral judgments. Their frameworks or models of general normative theory may ultimately mislead us if we slavishly declare allegiance to one and eschew the insights of the others. But if we reject general normative ethical theory altogether, we may be left with nothing but dizzying confusion in addressing moral questions. Given the importance of such questions, this is an option it would be silly, and perhaps dangerous, to pursue.

Our major focus in Part II of this book will be the exploration of several general normative theories. But we shall begin, in the remainder of Part I, with some basic questions of meta-ethics as these pertain to the very nature or status of morality. We shall explore the question of whether morality can in some manner be derived from either God's commands, cultural norms, individual emotional responses, or the terms of a social contract. We will be concerned with practical or applied ethics only to the extent that one often needs concrete cases and issues to illustrate the general directions in which the more abstract normative and meta-ethical theories take us. Frameworks are useful, but they tell us little unless we have some idea of their implications for real-life moral decision-making.

Notes

1. St. Augustine, *Confessions*, xi, 17.

2. Hobbes, *Leviathan* (1651), Library of Liberal Arts edn., (Indianapolis: Bobbs-Merrill, 1958) Part I, ch. 13, p. 107.

3. Unless the context makes plain a difference in meaning, we will employ the term "standards" as short for "moral principles, rules, values and ideals."

4. For an immensely challenging critique of modern ethical theory, and a call for a return to the approach advocated by Aristotle, see Alasdair MacIntyre, *After Virtue*, 2nd ed. (Notre Dame, Indiana: University of Notre Dame Press, 1984).

5. John Stuart Mill, *On Liberty*, Shields edn. (Indianapolis: Bobbs-Merrill, 1956), 56.

6. Aristotle, *Nicomachean Ethics*, trans. J.L. Ackrill (New York: Humanities Press, 1973), 1094 b12, 18.

7. As we saw above, such judgments can usually be distinguished from legal, prudential and aesthetic judgments, and from simple judgments of taste.

Two
Some Basics

Among the many virtues of good philosophical thinking is clarity. It is always important to be clear on the meaning of one's terms and any distinctions one wishes to draw. This is true whether one is studying the theory of knowledge, logic, metaphysics, the philosophy of law—or moral philosophy, which in no way stands as an exception. It will be useful, then, to consider some basic terminology commonly employed in ethical theory.

Judgments of Obligation

Judgments of obligation are typically made when we mean in some way to assess **conduct** or **actions**. In expressing such judgments we do not always use the word "obligation." As we will understand the phrase, judgments of obligation can be expressed using a variety of moral terms. Here are some examples:

- You **ought** to take all steps to save as many human lives as you can.

- Your overriding **duty** was to avoid intentionally harming people by your own hand.

- In creating and destroying those embryos for the purpose of stem cell research, you violated a fundamental **obligation** to respect the sanctity of human life.

- It was **right** for Spiro to keep his promise to the children; it would have been **wrong** not to do so.

- Your patients have **a right** to your utmost effort, care and concern.

- I **must** keep my promise.

- Bob **should** not have offered that bribe, even though it is the accepted practice.

Although only one of these sentences actually employs the word "obligation" explicitly, each one expresses what we will call a judgment of obligation. What unites judgments of obligation is that they all have to do directly with **conduct**: with how we should, or should not, **behave**. In short, they all concern the moral assessment of our **actions**.

Judgments of Value

Judgments of value, by contrast, are not, at least directly, about our actions. These are not assessments of what we should do, but about what things or properties are **good** or have **value**. For instance, the judgment that freedom is a good thing for human beings to enjoy or that pleasure is, in the end, the only thing of ultimate or intrinsic worth is a judgment of value. It does not tell us what we should do. Rather it tells us what things are good or valuable and possibly worthy of pursuit and promotion.

Judgments of Virtue

Among the many things often said to be of moral value are traits of character or dispositions traditionally called **moral virtues**. Typically, the moral virtues are thought to include traits like loyalty, honesty, kindness, courage, temperance and so on. Contrasted with the virtues are, of course, **vices**. These are typically thought to include cruelty, arrogance, intemperance, cowardice and so on. In the view of many, a moral person is best viewed, not as one whose actions comport with the right moral rules, but as one who leads a virtuous life. Compare the following two claims:

A. George's lie was morally wrong.

B. George is a dishonest person.

A deals with a particular action; **B** with the kind of person George is, with his character. **A** expresses a judgment of obligation, **B** a judgment of virtue. Judgments of obligation are meant to answer the question "What should I **do?**" Judgments of virtue are typically meant to answer a very different question: "What kind of person should I **be?**" Should I be loyal, and if so why? Should I be an honest person, and if so how can I best display this in my life? In the view of some philosophers, it is a mistake to view morality as essentially consisting of a set of rules or principles which our actions must follow if we are to be moral. The moral life does not consist simply in observing the right rules. It is a **way of life**

which requires a particular unity of thought, disposition, action and feeling characteristic of a virtuous person.[1]

Moral Ideals and Supererogation

In assessing persons and their actions morally, we are often drawn to distinguish between conduct and lives which are, in some minimal sense, morally acceptable, and those which observe much higher standards. Here is an example. Among most people's moral commitments is the willingness to help the less fortunate. But the extent of this commitment can vary enormously. Consider the following four individuals each of whom is committed to helping the needy.

1. James, who donates 0.1 per cent of his yearly salary to worthy charities.

2. Jeremy, who does what James does, but also volunteers occasionally at the local hospice.

3. Judy who does what Jeremy does, but also spends every weekend volunteering at the local women's shelter.

4. Mother Theresa.

Each of these courses of conduct might be said to be moral, but by no means are they morally equivalent to one another. At the one extreme we have James' actions which (let's assume) observes a minimal standard of moral decency with which all persons can be expected to comply in some way or other. At the other extreme we find a saintly life of self-sacrifice which no one is **required** to lead, but which is nonetheless highly praiseworthy. Mother Theresa's life was highly praiseworthy, morally speaking, but it went well beyond what morality **requires** of us, conceived of in terms of either duty or virtue. In short, her life exemplified a set of **moral ideals** at which the rest of us should aim, perhaps to lesser and varying degrees (as displayed by the conduct of Jeremy and Judy), but which we can seldom, if ever, be faulted for failing to achieve. In marking the distinction between that which is required, and that which, though praiseworthy, valuable, and worthy of pursuit and emulation, cannot be required, philosophers use the term **supererogation**. A supererogatory act is one which satisfies a moral ideal lying above the normal requirements of morality. The passerby who throws himself on a live bomb to save the many strangers who would otherwise be killed performs a supererogatory act—one which lives up to a moral ideal of courage and self-sacrifice to which many aspire, few achieve, and with which none can be required to comply.

Teleological or Consequentialist Theories of Obligation

Under some ethical theories judgments of obligation are dependent on, and follow directly from, judgments of value. Once we identify X as that which is good or valuable, these theories instruct us to pursue X. For example, some simple forms of utilitarianism claim that our moral duty is always to maximize the total amount of human happiness brought about by our actions. On such a theory, the judgment of obligation: "You are under a moral obligation to do X," follows directly from the judgment of value: "Doing X will create more human happiness than doing anything else." If an ethical theory asserts that judgments of obligation are dependent in this way on judgments of value, then it is what philosophers call a **teleological** or **consequentialist** theory of obligation. A consequentialist theory of obligation posits one and only one fundamental obligation, usually to **maximize** the good consequences and **minimize** the bad consequences of our conduct. Any other obligations we might be said to have, like Spiro's obligation to keep his promise to the kids, or Bob's obligation not to offer the bribe, are thought to be in some way derivable from this one fundamental obligation. According to a consequentialist we ought normally to keep our promises because doing so will almost always allow us to maximize good consequences. Since we need to know, under a consequentialist theory of obligation, which consequences are good so that we can promote them, and which are bad so that we can minimize them, it is easy to see why a teleological theory of obligation presupposes a **theory of value**. The latter theory will provide us with the basis upon which we can justify our judgments of value, and thus ultimately our judgments of obligation.

Deontological Theories of Obligation

In contrast to consequentialist theories of obligation are those which are said to be **deontological** in nature.[2] Deontological theories of obligation essentially deny what consequentialist theories assert: that we have one and only one fundamental duty, which is to maximize the good and minimize the bad consequences of our actions. In the view of the deontologist, there can be features of an action, besides its good or bad consequences, which bear directly on its moral rightness or wrongness. Consider again the momentous decision whether to bring down a hijacked airliner destined to crash into a densely populated office building. It is reasonably easy to see how a simple consequentialist approach, which

directs us to maximize the good and minimize the bad consequences of our actions, might lead to the conclusion that the
President should order the military to destroy the jet. Many
innocent lives—and all the human happiness associated with
them—will either be lost or profoundly affected by this military action. But thousands more will be similarly affected if
the action is not taken, thus leading to the difficult, though
inescapable, conclusion that the jet must be brought down.
If our moral obligation is always, in every situation in which
we are called on to act, to maximize the good and minimize
the bad consequences of what we do, there may be no other
option open to the President.

But some will balk at this line of reasoning, suggesting
that there are crucial features of the President's moral dilemma which are ignored by this consequentialist line of thinking.
Sometimes the very **nature** of the act, or the **intentions** with
which it is performed, can make an important difference. It
matters **how** consequences are brought about: it matters, for
example, whether we bring them about ourselves, or whether
they are produced by others whom we might have prevented
from acting. In other words, **intentionally** bringing about
bad consequences is not equivalent to **foreseeing** that bad
consequences will follow one's choice not to act, a point
which is ignored entirely if we restrict ourselves to toting up
consequences.[3]

Strong and Mixed Deontological Theories

Deontological theories of obligation deny, then, that the only
things that count in the moral assessment of actions are their
good and bad consequences. There are basically two forms
which this denial can take. First, a theory can suggest that
the good and bad consequences of our conduct have ab-

solutely no bearing whatsoever on their moral assessment. Such a theory, which we will call a **strong deontological theory**, can operate wholly independently of a theory of value. The reason is simple: our duty is not to maximize what is ultimately of value, and so we need not have a theory which tells us what that is. Kant, as we will see later in Chapter 7, appears to advocate a strong deontological theory of obligation.

A deontological theory of obligation need not, however, follow Kant's lead in denying the relevance of consequences altogether. There is a second, and perhaps much more plausible, kind of deontological theory which makes the far weaker claim that consequences are not the **only** factors of moral relevance. In other words, we have other ultimate obligations in addition to our duty to maximize good and minimize bad consequences. According to the **mixed deontological theory** of W.D. Ross the principle of beneficence, which requires promoting the good of others in our actions, is only one of many ultimate principles determining our moral obligations. Others include the principle requiring us to display gratitude for benefits given and the principle of fairness. In the view of deontologists who follow Ross's lead we sometimes have a duty to express our gratitude even when neglecting that duty would, on some particular occasion, lead to the best consequences. Such displays of gratitude can be morally obligatory regardless of whether they promote the best consequences. And some actions, for example, intentionally killing people with the aim of preventing many more from dying at the hands of hijackers, can be wrong despite the fact that they dramatically reduce bad consequences. Often these claims of the deontologist are expressed using the terminology of rights. People have rights, it is claimed, which often "trump" considerations of good and bad consequences. In other words, it is sometimes morally wrong to violate someone's rights, even when doing so will lead to the best consequences overall.

Pluralist and Monistic Theories of Obligation

As we have just seen, Ross is unlike Mill and Kant in suggesting that we have many fundamental moral obligations. The duty to express gratitude and the duty to be fair are, for Ross, ultimate obligations which are not based on, or derivable from, any more basic principle of obligation like Mill's principle of utility or Kant's Categorical Imperative. This clearly sets Ross apart from Mill and Kant. Mill, for example, would agree that we frequently have a duty to be fair. But he would insist that this is only because observing the practice of always acting fairly towards others allows us to fulfil our ultimate obligation, which is to maximize the balance of good over bad consequences. But Ross will have none of this. For him the duty to be fair is just as ultimate as the duty to maximize good consequences. Ross's theory is an example of what we will call a **pluralistic theory of obligation**. Putting it simply, such a theory is one which does not posit a single, fundamental obligation (or principle) in relation to which all other obligations (or principles) are secondary or derivative. This defining feature raises a serious difficulty for one who advocates a pluralistic theory of obligation: What are we to do in situations where our ultimate obligations appear to conflict with one another? Without some means of adjudicating among conflicting obligations, a pluralistic theory of obligation contains a serious gap. It fails, in the end, to help us determine what to do.[4]

A **monistic theory of obligation** avoids this difficulty of conflicting obligations by positing one fundamental obligation, and one corresponding rule or principle defining that obligation. Examples include the principle of utility, the categorical imperative, and possibly the principle of fairness. A utilitarian, as we have noted, will be happy to talk of obligations to tell the truth or to be fair to other people in our dealings with them. He will simply add that we have these obligations only because being fair and telling the truth usually lead, in the end and with all relevant factors considered, to the best consequences overall. And if two or more of these obligations conflict in a particular case—say when telling the truth would produce unfairness—then we must resort to the principle of utility and determine which obligation to respect. This is because our fundamental or primary obligation is always to maximize the good and minimize the bad consequences of our action. Utilitarianism, then, is a monistic theory of obligation. So too is Kant's strong deontological theory.

Pluralist and Monistic Theories of Value

When we turn to theories of value, we find that these too may be categorized as either monistic or pluralistic. A **monistic** theory of value, as one might expect, posits one and only one thing, property, quality or characteristic of things, as valuable for its own sake. In other words, it posits one and only one thing as **intrinsically valuable**. **Hedonism** is one historically influential type of monistic theory of value. On this view **pleasure** is the only thing which is valuable for its own sake. Anything else that we value, say money or friendship, is valuable only **instrumentally**, as a means to the pleasure it brings. Classical utilitarianism, of the form espoused by Mill and his mentor Jeremy Bentham, provides one example of a hedonistic theory of value. But utilitarianism need not be wedded to hedonism. The English philosopher, G.E. Moore, was a utilitarian like Mill. But unlike Mill he espoused a **pluralistic theory of value** which viewed pleasure as only one of many things which have intrinsic or non-instrumental value. Knowledge and aesthetic experience are among many other things worthy of pursuit for their own sake.[5] If one holds a pluralistic theory of value, then one is faced with the same kind of difficulty encountered by pluralistic theories of obligations: What are we to say about situations where two or more values or valuable things are in competition with one another? Is comparing knowledge and pleasure, so as to see which is of greater value or importance in the circumstances, something that can be done rationally—i.e., with the backing of good reasons? Is an attempt to compare these two valuable things a bit like trying to compare apples and oranges?[6]

Monistic theories of value may seem preferable on this particular score, but the appearance may be largely illusory. We may only have to compare, say, one person's pleasure with that of another, as hedonism requires, but it is far from clear how this is to be done. How do we compare one person's pleasure with that of another? What kind of scale would we use? We can compare temperatures by using a thermometer, but there is no comparable device to measure amounts of pleasure. So it is difficult to get a handle on how such **inter-personal comparisons of pleasure** (or utility) could be done—especially if the persons involved are as different as, say, Pope John Paul II and Mick Jagger.

Monistic theories of value face another, perhaps even more fundamental, objection. Many people follow Moore's lead in suggesting that there are numerous things in the world of ultimate, irreducible value. Does one understand friendship, for example, if one attempts to reduce its value to the pleasure it brings? If one thinks of a friend as one whose value **depends** on the pleasure one derives from the friendship, then has one really grasped what it is to be a friend? Perhaps the same can be said of a parent's relationship with her children? If we say that Marcie finds her children valuable only to the extent that they increase her pleasure, have we grasped the nature of the child/parent relationship? Have we not in fact got things backwards? Marcie experiences great pleasure in seeing her children thrive **because she values them**. She does not value them **because of the pleasure they bring her** (at least sometimes!). If these observations are correct, then it would seem that there is more of value in the world than pleasure, things like friendship and the valuable relationships we have with our children. If so, then it seems implausible to suppose that a monistic theory of moral value could be valid.

The Language of Rights

As noted earlier, judgments of obligation can be expressed in any number of ways, using any number of moral terms. These include terms like "ought," "duty," "obligation," "should," "required," "must" and so on. At one time in the history of moral thinking, the terms "duty," "ought" and "obligation" were the ones most commonly used in rendering judgments of obligation. But today there is little doubt that our moral vocabulary is dominated by the language of rights. Instead of saying "You ought not to have done X," or "Your responsibility was to have done X rather than Y," a speaker is more apt to say "You had no **right** to do that," or "You were wrong to do that because you violated your neighbour's **rights**." But what is the cause of this change from "obligation-talk" to "rights-talk" and what, if anything, does it signal?

Two :: *Some Basics*

The factors responsible for this shift in vocabulary are difficult to specify. No doubt they are numerous and multi-faceted, and subject to considerable controversy among cultural historians, sociologists and other empirical social scientists. But one important factor may have been a paradigm shift in western **political** culture away from viewing people as subject to the will of political authorities like kings and queens, and towards viewing them as bearers of rights against these political rulers. Although morality and politics are not identical, there is no doubt that they strongly influence one another, and there is little reason to think that this is not the case in the shift from obligation-talk to rights-talk. So let's do a little speculative cultural history.

At one point in the development of western culture it was widely believed that citizens owed obligations to kings and queens because the latter ruled by "divine right." That is, it was widely believed that we owe political and moral obligations to our rulers, that we are their "subjects," because they rule by the authority of God. On this conception, the person is not the subject of political entitlements. Rather, she is subject to the will of another—she owes them obedience. This conception of political authority gave way, in the seventeenth and eighteenth centuries, to what is commonly called the "social contract theory." On this theory, as articulated by great political thinkers like John Locke and Thomas Hobbes, political authority is not granted by God to kings and queens to be exercised at will over subjects.[7] On the contrary, it is the subjects themselves who invest their rulers with authority, by way of a social contract. On this latter conception of political authority the locus of legitimacy switches from the ruler (and God) towards the individual citizen. She is the one with primary moral and political standing, the one who has **natural rights** which cannot be sacrificed without her consent.

Once the individual becomes in this way the locus of political legitimacy, and once we go from thinking of individuals as subject to requirements imposed by others, towards thinking of them as possessing political and moral entitlements which their rulers must respect, our whole focus shifts. We move from "obligation talk" to "rights talk."

Whether these changes in perspective and vocabulary bring with them different judgments of obligation—not just the same judgments expressed in different ways—is a difficult question which we cannot fully address here. But it is not unreasonable to think that the shift towards viewing the **individual** as the bearer of rights might well have been accompanied by a corresponding shift in people's moral judgments both inside and outside the political context. As we have seen, the move from subject to participant in a contract is significant, and brings with it a completely different way of viewing our relationship with government. But this change in perspective could easily have had an effect outside the political context as well. It is not hard to imagine a corresponding drift towards accepting deontological theories which typically assert that there are things one cannot do to an individual—like sacrifice his or her life in order to save a greater number of lives—because to do so would violate that individual's rights. Whether this shift in direction actually occurred is a question which cannot be explored fully here. But the possibility is worth bearing in mind as we consider the variety of moral theories explored below, especially utilitarianism which is rejected by many contemporary ethical theorists. One of the most common complaints against utilitarianism is that it fails to recognize and respect the importance of individual rights.[8]

So contemporary morality and politics are dominated by the vocabulary of rights. But the language of rights is complex and often confusing, if only because the term "rights" can be used to designate any one of a number of different normative (e.g., moral, legal or political) relationships. In order to facilitate clarity of thought and deliberation, we need to sort out some of these differences. The conceptual map which follows is largely derived from the theory of legal rights proposed in the early twentieth century by the American legal scholar, Wesley Hohfeld and from the more recent account of moral rights developed by the contemporary philosopher Joel Feinberg.[9]

Claim Rights

What is a right? On what does it rest? According to Hohfeld, a right is, strictly speaking, an enforceable claim to someone else's action or non-action. That rights are in some sense **enforceable** claims is one reason why the language of rights seems so natural within the realm of law. If one has a right to X, then one can demand X as one's due, and if the right is a legal one, then one is usually entitled to the enforcement of that right through the coercive power of the law. Of course rights are not restricted to law. It is quite natural, for example, to speak of moral rights to such things as the keeping of promises or the assistance of our friends. Generally speaking, when one has a rightful claim to X, it is not merely good, or desirable, or preferable that one should have X; one is entitled to it and another person (or group of persons) has a correlative duty or obligation to respect one's entitlement.[10] For instance, I have both a moral and legal right not to be assaulted by you. This entails not that it would be a good or desirable thing were you to refrain from assaulting me, but that you are under both a moral and legal obligation not to assault me. This kind of right, a claim against other people, is what Hohfeld calls a **claim-right**. A claim-right is always paired with a corresponding duty or obligation which applies to at least one other person. Violation of my claim-right is always the violation, by someone else, of his or her duty towards me.[11]

Claim rights come in a variety of different forms. In sorting these out, Joel Feinberg develops three helpful distinctions:

    (i)   in personam versus in rem rights

    (ii)   positive versus negative rights

    (iii)   passive versus active rights.

    (i) In personam rights are said to hold against one or more determinate, specifiable persons. These are determinate persons who are under corresponding or correlative obligations. For example, if Spiro owes his children some ice cream, then there are specifiable persons against whom the children enjoy their moral claim-right. Other examples, some from within the legal domain, include: rights under contract; rights of landlords to payment of rent from their tenants; the right against one's employer to a safe and healthy working environment; the moral right to one's physician's best professional judgment and care; the moral right to be told the truth in the course of our everyday interactions with people; and the moral right to the concern and respect of our friends and colleagues. Examples of possible in personam claim-rights around which deep moral controversy revolve include: the right of a fetus not to be harmed by the conduct of the woman who carries it; the right to the assistance of one's physician in taking one's own life in the latter stages of a terminal illness; and perhaps the right of grown children to the continued financial support of their parents.

Not all claim-rights are held against specifiable persons. Some hold against people generally. This kind of right, called an **in rem right**, is said to hold against "the world at large." For instance, my right not to be assaulted holds not against any particular person or persons, but against anyone and everyone who might be in a position to commit such an offence against me. This includes my neighbours, people at bus stops, terrorists, and surgeons who might be tempted to operate on me in a non-emergency situation without first gaining my consent. All persons are under both a moral and a legal obligation not to assault me which is paired with my in rem right not to be assaulted by them. Other possible examples of in rem rights include: the right to an unpolluted natural environment; the right to express oneself freely; and the right to one's personal religious beliefs. More controversial examples include: the moral right to a minimum level of subsistence; an unfettered legal right to the practice of one's religion, even when this involves harmful activities, like refusing, for religious reasons, consent to a life-saving blood transfusion for one's child; the legal right to make, distribute and consume pornographic materials; the legal right to undergo an abortion; and the moral right to the assistance of others when either one's life or one's welfare is in serious danger.

(ii) **Positive** and **negative rights** form another subclass of claim-rights. A positive right is a right to someone else's positive action. A negative right, on the other hand, is a right to another person's non-action or forbearance. If someone enjoys a positive right to something, this means that there is at least one other person who has an obligation actually to do something, usually to the first person's benefit. My dependent children have a positive right, both moral and legal, that I provide them with the necessities of life. This requires that I do lots of different things, like provide them with food and shelter, ensure that they have essential educational opportunities, and so on. If, on the other hand, a right is negative, this means that there is at least one other person who is under obligation to refrain from doing something which would be detrimental to the right-holder's interests. My children have a negative right not to be unreasonably prevented from listening to music they enjoy. This means (regrettably) that I must refrain from turning up my Van Morrison in order to drown out my son's acid Jazz. But because the right is negative, not positive, it (thankfully) does not require that I actually buy his CDs for him.

(iii) Depending on what it is that the other person(s) must refrain from doing, a negative right can be either passive or active. **Active rights** are negative rights to go about one's own business free from the interference of others. We might call these **freedom rights**. Paired with freedom rights are **duties of non-interference**, as when I must refrain from cutting the electricity supply to my son's stereo. Some women who claim a right to abortion, are asserting a right not to be interfered with or hindered in their efforts to secure an abortion. Corresponding to such an active right is the duty on the part of governments (and any other persons of power and/or influence) not to hinder women in these efforts. Laws which make it a criminal offence to procure an abortion are said by many to violate this duty, and to infringe on a woman's correlative active right to non-interference in acting on their personal reproductive decisions.

An active freedom right is a right **to do** something, free from interference. **Passive negative rights**, on the other hand, are rights not to have certain things **done to us**. They involve **freedom from** (the undesirable or harmful effects of other people's activities) not **freedom to** (do or not do certain things ourselves). We might, for convenience, refer to these as **security rights,** rights to be secure against the harmful or undesirable effects of other people's conduct. Obvious examples include the right not to be killed or assaulted, and the right not to be inflicted with disease and injury by negligent health care professionals. Other, more controversial, examples include a proposed right not to be exposed to offensive pornography; a right not to be exposed to blasphemous speech; a right against the destruction of one's culture, religion or language; and a right to be free from terror. Each of these involves, not a right against interference with one's own activities, but rather a right not to suffer the effects of other people's activities.

It is well worth noting that typically active freedom rights of non-interference can be protected only at the expense of other people's passive security rights. The active freedom right of a manufacturer to pursue a livelihood within the capitalist system often competes with the passive, in personam, security rights of workers. It also competes with the passive, in rem rights of the community or world at large not to have its environment fouled by industrial activities. One of the central problems of moral, legal and political philosophy is how to balance the active, freedom rights of one set of individuals against the passive security rights of others. For example, to what extent should certain civil liberties—e.g., the right to travel and associate freely—be curtailed in times of global crisis when acts of terrorism threaten the lives and security of the world's citizens? Different people will place differing emphases on the competing rights. The resolution of such difficult questions is neither clear nor easy and typically marks different political philosophies and approaches. Libertarians, for example, emphasize the importance of freedom rights; some communitarians, on the other hand, applaud the protection of community interests against the harmful effects of rampant individualism.

To sum up, claim-rights can be either in personam or in rem, positive or negative, and if they are negative, they can be either passive (security rights) or active (freedom rights). Correlated with any one of these rights is always a duty or obligation on the part of at least one other person. Claim-rights are claims against others who are under duty to respect them.

Liberties or Privileges

When we speak of rights we most often have claim-rights in mind. But this is not always the case. Sometimes the situations in which people assert or are granted rights do not involve claims against other people who are under correlative obligations. Rather, they involve what Hohfeld called **privileges** or **liberties**. My having a privilege does not entail that anyone else is under obligation towards me. Rather it entails only the **absence** of an obligation on **my** part. If I enjoy the privilege of doing (or not doing) something, then I am free or at liberty to do it (or not do it) and I do no wrong, violate no obligation, should I exercise that privilege. In short, a privilege is the absence of, or freedom from, duty. An example from the law may help to clarify the nature of a privilege and illustrate how it differs from, in particular, active freedom rights.

In most legal systems there is a standing duty to provide the court with whatever information it requests. One must provide that information even if one would prefer not to do so, or if it is in one's interest to remain silent. However, many jurisdictions also recognize a special context in which this standing duty does not apply. They recognize a right—a privilege—against self-incrimination. What this means is that in this special area, i.e., evidence which may implicate me in a crime, I am at liberty to decline the court's request for information. In this special case I cannot be compelled to testify if I choose not to do so. But notice, if I have no claim-right against self-incrimination, but only a privilege, and if a sharp lawyer somehow gets me to say something which does in fact incriminate me, then I have no basis for complaint. He has not violated my rights. A violation would have occurred only if my right were a claim-right against him. Were it a claim-right, then the lawyer would be under a corresponding duty or obligation not to trick me into incriminating myself. But with privileges there are no such corresponding duties, only the absence of duty on my part. I am at liberty to act (or not act) but this liberty does not enjoy the protection of corresponding duties or obligations on the part of other people to respect my liberty. Privileges are what we might call **unprotected liberties**. In this respect they are very unlike negative claim-rights whose freedoms are always protected by corresponding obligations. Such claim-rights, whether active or passive, are always **protected freedoms**.[12]

Situations in which the right asserted is a privilege are not as obvious as those involving claim-rights. But they do exist outside the context of the right against self-incrimination. One familiar example is any situation in which I provide informed **consent** to have something done which would, absent my consent, have resulted in the violation of my rights. Take the common practice of gaining the **informed consent** of patients before embarking on surgical procedures. By providing consent to surgery a patient waives his claim-right not to be "touched" by the surgeon, thereby relieving or freeing the latter of her otherwise standing duty not to touch the patient. In short, he grants the surgeon a privilege without which any act of touching would amount to assault or battery.

Other examples can be found in the increasingly important areas of **privacy** and **confidentiality**. These notions are becoming increasingly important because of the rapidly expanding degree to which information about us is so easily collected, circulated and used for unwarranted purposes by government bodies, financial institutions, corporations wanting to sell us their products, prospective employers and so on. Certain individuals are legally (and perhaps morally) exempt from duties to respect certain confidential or private information about us. Certain health care professionals, for example, are privileged with respect to confidential information about our medical history. Access to such private, confidential information is something from which the general public is barred. Members of the general public are under a duty to respect the confidentiality of our medical records; they have no right to these privileged items, access to which would violate our right to privacy. Those under whose care we place ourselves are, however, privileged. They are exempt from this otherwise standing duty to keep away from this information. It would be highly misleading to say that these health care workers have a claim to my medical records. It is not at all misleading, however, to say that they are at liberty to inspect them if I place myself under their care.

The notion of privileged information is not, of course, restricted to the health care context. Take, for example, the liberty to examine my bank records that I grant my financial counsellor, or the mortgage officer from whom I wish to secure a loan. Or consider the privilege I grant a prospective employer to inquire about my employment history or do a background criminal check on me. In each instance I grant someone the liberty of doing what would otherwise amount to a violation of my rights. I exempt her from an otherwise standing duty not to seek out or possess confidential, privileged information about me.

It is perhaps worth stressing again that privileges are always **unprotected** liberties. Contrast a situation in which a patient grants his physician the privilege of examining his confidential medical records with a situation involving the Medical Officer of Health. The Medical Officer may well have a legally enforceable claim-right to examine the relevant files, say for the purposes of tracking a highly infectious disease. If so, then the patient, and perhaps the hospital or physician's office in which those files are housed, have a duty to provide access to the required information. They have a duty or obligation to turn the files over and do wrong if they should fail to do so. If, on the other hand, the patient simply forgets to arrange for his records to reach the physician's hand, he has in no way violated the latter's rights. This is because the physician has been granted a mere privilege, not a claim-right with its corresponding duty.

Powers

Sometimes the language of rights is used to describe neither a claim-right nor a privilege. In some situations where a person is said to have the right to do X, what is meant is that he has a **normative power**. A normative power is the capacity to bring about some change in an existing pattern of rights, duties, and privileges. In short, it is **the capacity to alter existing normative relationships**. Perhaps the most clear-cut context in which powers are exercised involve **agency**—when one party, the agent, acts on behalf of another party, the client, in bringing about changes to the normative relationships the client has with other people. Suppose I empower my lawyer to sign a contract on my behalf. What this means is that the lawyer can now place me under a contractual obligation by signing the contract in my place. He has the power to bring about that change in my normative relationships, to place me under duty to honour a claim against me which will, in virtue of the lawyer's actions, be possessed by my contractual partner. The latter now has a right to whatever it is that my lawyer said I would provide. Of course, he also has an obligation to provide whatever it was he promised to provide in return. In this context of legal agency the lawyer has the capacity to alter my existing normative situation and to bring about a new constellation of claim-rights and duties. In describing this power we sometimes say that I have granted him the right to act on my behalf, by which we mean, not that he has a claim-right against me, but that he now has the power to alter my normative commitments.

Although they play a central role in strictly legal contexts, such as the law of contracts, powers are evident in many other contexts as well. Take, once again, the practice of medicine and the role of a **surrogate decision-maker**. If I am incapacitated, a member of my family may have the legal and moral right to make medical decisions on my behalf. If she exercises this right, the surrogate can alter the normative relationship between me and a physician by granting the latter the right to perform surgery on me. In so doing the surrogate would be exercising a power to relieve the physician of her otherwise standing duty not to touch me. Put another way, the surrogate waives my claim-right not to have my body invaded. Without the exercise of this power, the surgeon's actions would, as we have seen, amount to assault and/or battery. Of course in most contexts patients themselves exercise the power of consent. But when for some reason they are unable to do so, a surrogate is normally sought to act on their behalf—a surrogate who exercises the power which otherwise resides in the individual patient.

A less obvious, but equally important, context in which normative power is exercised is the making of promises. In making a promise to bring some ice cream home for the kids, Spiro places himself under a moral obligation to do so. Of course, he also invests the kids with a claim-right to the goodies. In exercising the powers associated with promising, we attempt to alter the normative status quo: that is, we attempt to change existing rights and obligations. And we normally do so, except in those rare cases where what we promise to do is something it would be wrong for us to do. If I "promise" my wife that I will steal a sport utility vehicle for her, I have not, despite my efforts, altered the normative status quo. She is not, in virtue of my "promise," now entitled to the SUV. This is because the power to bind ourselves by promising does not extend to immoral conduct. Since stealing is something I am not entitled to do, I cannot place myself under a moral obligation to do it. As this example illustrates, normative powers, such as the powers of agency, surrogacy or promising, are all subject to limits or boundaries. Step outside those boundaries and one's attempt to alter the normative status quo fails. Where exactly the boundaries lie in any particular case can be a very difficult question to answer.

Concluding Thoughts on the Language of Rights

One should always be alert when one encounters rights-talk. It is important to ask whether the right asserted is a claim-right or only a privilege. These are different conceptually and have very different implications. If only a privilege is asserted, then there will be no one else who is under a corresponding duty or obligation. Not so, however, if the right in question is a claim-right. Here there is always someone under a corresponding duty. If a claim-right is being asserted, then one should always ask whether it is in rem or in personam. Is there some particular person who is said to be under the corresponding duty, or is the right supposed to hold against the world at large? Take, for example, a right to the bare necessities of life. Sometimes when this right is asserted, we have in mind particular governments or groups against whom the right is asserted. The right to subsistence would, in this context, be held against one's government or family. But at other times, the speaker might intend to express the view that **all of us**, wherever we are and whatever our circumstances, have an obligation to see to the welfare of our fellow human beings. This latter right might form the basis of an argument in favour of donating to Oxfam or in favour of generous foreign aid policies. It could also be the basis for an argument demanding the cessation of practices undertaken by developed countries which threaten the food supplies of less developed nations. In these instances, the duties entailed do not apply to specific, identifiable persons or groups. They apply to all of us as members of the human community.

When claim-rights are asserted, it may also be crucial to be clear whether what is being claimed is a positive or a negative right. Is the claim only that others refrain from doing something, or is positive action being demanded? The difference between these two claims can be enormous, if only because taking positive action is often (though not always) much more costly than refraining from action. One famous instance in which the difference proved crucial was the United State Supreme Court's decision in **Roe v Wade**. This decision was interpreted by some to mean that the court had recognized a positive right to abortion, which entailed an obligation on the part of government to provide facilities and financial assistance for women seeking abortions. A 1977 ruling, however, made it clear that while it was unconstitutional for the state to prevent women from having elective abortions, this in no way entailed a government obligation to facilitate such activities. In other words, the 1977 ruling made plain that the right granted was a negative freedom right, not a positive right to the assistance of government in exercising that right.

The difference between positive and negative rights is as vital in ethical (and political) theory as it is in law. Some theories emphasize negative freedom rights and minimize the importance and force of positive rights. Many libertarian thinkers, for example, stress the liberty or privilege of pursuing one's own interests free from any positive duties to provide for others. These others, of course, have an equal liberty to pursue their own interests. Libertarian thinkers also give great weight to the protections afforded by negative freedom rights to non-interference. Many applaud free market economies which are, in their view, corrupted by misguided state intervention in the name of positive rights. Theories of this sort find great appeal in the idea of the individual's unconstrained (but protected) freedom to pursue her own interests and projects as she sees fit and as she defines them. The fundamental purpose of law and morality, on this view, is the protection and enhancement of individual liberty.

Towards the other end of the spectrum of moral and political theory are those willing to assert the importance of the general good, and the importance of positive rights to assistance from other people. Utilitarians who wish to employ the language of rights will generally be prepared to affirm positive rights when their observance generally serves to maximize the general good, i.e., utility. On such theories, it is terribly wrong merely to leave people to their own devices. We are morally required to concern ourselves with their interests, and sometimes to sacrifice our own liberties and freedoms for theirs. How far one must go in doing so is a crucial question upon which the plausibility of many utilitarian theories depends.

The Meaning of Moral Judgments: Cognitivism vs Non-Cognitivism

The above reflections amply demonstrate that there are many different kinds of moral judgment: judgments about obligations, about values, and those which concern worthy moral ideals. They also reveal that moral philosophers differ significantly in both the structure and the details of their general normative theories: some theories are teleological, others deontological; some stress rights, others duties or obligations. Yet another topic about which moral philosophers disagree is the very **meaning** of moral judgments, whether these are judgments of obligation, judgments of value, or what have you. The first half of the twentieth century was dominated by meta-ethical disputes surrounding this question and saw the development of two radically different approaches to the meaning of moral utterances.

Cognitivists hold that moral utterances typically purport to assert true moral propositions which can be grasped and judged by way of our cognitive faculties. Although the types of reasons offered to support the following two judgments would no doubt be different, a cognitivist will insist that "The Pope lives in Rome" and "Hitler's policies concerning the Jewish people were morally wrong" each expresses a true proposition. Furthermore, he will insist that the truth of each of these two propositions is, at least in theory, capable of demonstration. The first purports to describe a **physical** fact about the world and would be backed up by empirical evidence. The second asserts a **moral** fact, which would be supported by the offering of moral reasons. But in each instance the person intends to express an "objective truth" which is capable both of being grasped and understood and of being supported by appropriate reasons or evidence.

Some philosophers find cognitivism highly problematic for a number of reasons. Among the most influential is the claim that there is widespread disagreement on most moral questions. Indeed, there is little agreement on how we should go about trying to answer moral questions! Some people are consequentialists, others are deontologists. Some emphasize rights, others virtues. If moral judgments do assert propositions capable of being judged as true or false, then would we not expect to see far greater consensus on moral questions? Would we not at least have more agreement on how to go about trying to achieve consensus?[13] For these and other reasons, philosophers like A.J. Ayer, C.L. Stevenson, and R.M. Hare developed alternative **non-cognitivist** theories about the meaning of moral utterances.

Non-Cognitivism 1: A.J. Ayer's Emotivism

Ayer's view, as articulated in his influential book, **Language Truth and Logic**, was perhaps the most extreme of the three.[14] It was certainly the simplest. Ayer held that moral utterances simply express the emotions of the speaker. For that reason alone they are non-cognitive in nature. My saying "Abortion is wrong" is rather like my saying "Abortion—Boo!!" I express my negative emotion towards the practice of abortion in much the same way as when I yell "Boo!!" following the goalie's having surrendered the fifth straight goal of the period. One must be careful here: there is a crucial difference between **expressing** an emotion and **stating** that one has it. Ayer's view is that moral utterances do the former, not the latter. If one held that the role of a moral utterance is to **state that** one has a particular emotion about subjects like abortion, lying, or attempting to exterminate the Jews of Europe, then moral judgments **would** express propositions capable of truth or falsity. A description of one's emotions is still a description, and can be judged accurate or inaccurate, true or false. But this is not Ayer's position.

Non-Cognitivism 2: C.L. Stevenson's Emotivism

Ayer's view was that moral utterances express but do not state our emotions. A similar view was held by C.L. Stevenson who, like Ayer, denied that moral utterances purport to describe anything at all, including one's emotions.[15] Stevenson suggested that moral utterances express the speaker's (positive or negative) non-cognitive **attitudes** and seek to evoke these same attitudes in the ones to whom the utterances are directed. When Stacey says to you "Stem cell research is morally wrong" she not only expresses her attitude of disapproval toward the practice. She also attempts to get you to share that attitude and be motivated to engage in behaviour designed to foster its elimination. Unlike Ayer who saw little if any role for moral reasoning, Stevenson seized on the fact that many of our attitudes are largely the product of what we believe to be true or false. As a result, a change in belief can often result in a corresponding change in attitude. Were you more fully apprised of the facts surrounding stem cell research, you might come to share Stacey's attitude of disapproval toward it. Since much reasoning is involved in attempts to substantiate or alter beliefs, much reasoning is involved in attempts to shift or solidify moral attitudes. Good moral reasoning is persuasive reasoning, that is reasoning which actually gets others to share the attitude of the speaker. But Stevenson was also of the view that there can come a point where reasons are no longer available. At this point the best we can do is just express our attitude. If, after as much persuasive effort as I could muster, someone were to say: "Yes, but I still don't see why I should care about another person's pain?" I may have no reply but to express my attitude of disapproval toward that state of affairs.

Non-Cognitivism 3: R.M. Hare's Prescriptivism

R.M. Hare, like Ayer and Stevenson, denied that moral utterances **describe** anything at all, including our emotions or attitudes. In this respect his theory may be described as noncognitivist in orientation. But, according to Hare, moral judgments do not express emotions or attitudes either. Rather they express **universal prescriptions**.[16] That is, they prescribe courses of conduct for anyone at all who finds him/herself in the type of circumstance in question. When Carrie says "Abortion after the second trimester is morally wrong" she asserts a universally applicable prescription which might be more perspicuously expressed as follows: "Do no abortion after the second trimester!" Such an assertion does not describe anything, nor does it necessarily express an emotion or attitude. Rather it tells us directly what to do, in much the same way as the doctor's prescription: "Take two pills every night before bed!" tells Rob what to do in order to get better. The doctor, in making his prescription, is not describing anything, nor is he expressing his attitudes or venting his emotions. He is providing an answer to an important question for Rob: "What shall I do to get better?" In Hare's view one who makes a moral utterance purports to answer a similar, but more basic and unqualified question. He purports to answer the question "What shall I do—period?" In Hare's view answers to this fundamental question of morality override answers to all others. The prescriptions of morality are, in his view, fully universal and cannot be overridden by other prescriptions (of law, custom, professional codes, accepted medical practice etc.)

Like Stevenson, Hare wishes to secure a place for reasoning in establishing moral conclusions. Just as reasons can (we hope!) always be given for a doctor's prescription, reasons should be available to support one's moral prescriptions. To this end Hare develops an elaborate theory of moral reasoning which requires us to test our willingness to accept the logical implications of our universal prescriptions. If I cannot accept these implications, then rationality and moral integrity require that I reject my prescription. And to reject the prescription is to refuse to act on it. Among the implications of my universal prescriptions will always be a willingness on my part to have everyone else who might find himself in exactly my situation act on my proposed prescription. If I am not willing to accept the universalization of my prescription to include all such situations, **including the ones in which I am the one on the "receiving" or "losing" end**, then I may not act on my prescription. As Hare goes on to show, this aspect of his theory puts him squarely in line with Immanuel Kant whose view we will explore in Part II below. It also captures an element of virtually every widely accepted moral code, **the Golden Rule**, that instructs us to do unto others as we would have them do unto us.

So, do moral utterances express propositions capable of truth value? This is a question to which no answer is readily available. But this need not deter us from exploring other dimensions of ethical theory. Whether or not our moral claims can ultimately be judged true or false, we do seem capable of assessing them, and judging them to be better or worse than others. So let us turn to some theories purporting to reveal the foundations upon which such judgments can be based.

Notes

1. The nature and role of the virtues will be explored more fully later, in Chapter 9, which deals with "virtue ethics."

2. The term "deontological" derives from the Greek word for duty, "deon." The term "teleological" derives from the Greek word "telos" which is the Greek translation for "goal."

3. For more on this, see Chapter 6 below.

4. On this see Chapter 8 below.

5. See G.E. Moore, *Principia Ethica* (London: Cambridge University Press, 1903).

6. These questions will be explored more fully below in Chapter 6.

7. For Locke's political theory, see his *Two Treatises of Government* (1690). Hobbes' classic work is *Leviathan* (1651). Numerous editions of both works are in print. The Hobbesian social contract theory of political authority will be examined later in Chapter 5.

8. This is denied by most contemporary utilitarians who attempt to find a place, within their utilitarian framework, for a set of robust moral rights. Rights are justified, on most utilitarian theories, because at the end of the day, respecting rights leads to the best consequences overall. See Chapter 6 below.

9. W. Hohfeld, *Fundamental Legal Conceptions* (New Haven: Yale University Press, 1919) and Joel Feinberg, "Duties, Rights and Claims," in *Rights, Justice and the Bounds of Liberty* (Princeton: Princeton University Press, 1980).

10. While there are exceptions, it is generally true that if X has a claim-right to A, then someone else has a corresponding duty or obligation of some kind — and vice versa. It is for this reason that the language of rights and the language of obligation are sometimes thought to be equivalent. But as noted in the previous section, the two vocabularies can be significantly different in the moral perspectives

with which they are associated. It is also not clear that all obligations entail corresponding rights.

11. Although the terms "duty" and "obligation" are sometimes treated as different in meaning—e.g., duties are sometimes thought to attach to official positions such as those of policeman, judge, and teacher—we will treat them as equivalent in meaning and use them interchangeably. And of course legal claim-rights can differ quite significantly in content from moral claim-rights. Though related in many ways, law and morality are different from one another. For example, one whose life is in peril may have a moral right to the assistance of a passerby who can easily effect a rescue. But in many legal jurisdictions there is no corresponding legal right. Despite these differences in content, and the different means of enforcement employed in law as opposed to morality, the basic structure of claim-rights is the same in both domains.

12. Recall that active claim-rights involve **freedom to** (do or not do certain things) while passive claim-rights involve **freedom from** (harmful or undesirable effects of other people's activities).

13. Closely related arguments (the Diversity and Demonstrability Arguments) in favour of a **moral relativism** will be explored in much greater detail below in Chapter 3. The responses given there can easily be modified to answer the argument presently being considered.

14. A.J. Ayer, *Language, Truth and Logic* (London: Victor Gollancz Ltd., 1936; New York: Dover Publications, 1950).

15. C.L. Stevenson, *Ethics and Language* (New Haven: Yale University Press, 1944).

16. Hare, *Freedom and Reason* (Oxford: Oxford University Press, 1963); *Moral Thinking* (Oxford: Oxford University Press, 1981).

Three
It's All Just Relative—
Or Is It?

Why Relativism?

When one explores the history of humankind, one cannot help but be struck by a profound lack of consensus on many moral questions. Different societies and cultures, and different people within one and the same society or culture, appear to have dramatically different moral beliefs and practices. The moralities of some societies demand that grown children make every reasonable effort to care for their elderly, dependent parents. The moral codes of other societies have permitted, indeed in some instances have required, that elderly, dependent parents be exposed to the elements so that nature may claim their lives and relieve their families of the burden of care. Some contemporary anti-abortionists reject abortion as murder. Other members of contemporary Western societies are "pro-choice" and condemn, as nothing short of slavery, legislation requiring women to bring their pregnancies to full term. In light of such deep differences in moral beliefs and practices, it is obvious to many that there are no universal, generally applicable moral principles, rules and values, valid for all times and places.[1] It is obvious, in other words, that morality has no objective, rational basis, that there are no "objective moral truths" upon which all reasonable people could be expected to agree were they fully aware of all the relevant facts and information. When it comes to morality, many say, "everything is relative."

This very popular position, which we will call **Moral Relativism**, is often thought to be the only view which takes seriously what we have learned about the many different moral practices of people around the world—and about the dangers of "moral imperialism." By this latter phrase is meant (1) the tendency to think and act as though our own moral views, or those of our society or culture, are obviously correct (or at least better); and (2) the belief that we are at liberty, perhaps under duty, to bring enlightenment to the confused and the mistaken. Some moral imperialists go one step further and require, if necessary, (3) forceful imposition of their superior moral views upon the recalcitrant. One does not have to be a moral relativist to see danger in moral imperialism. The courage of one's convictions is always best mixed with a measure of humility, and with a willingness to entertain the possibility that one's moral beliefs could be improved. But a moral relativist may be in the strongest position to underscore the often unfounded assumptions underlying the imperialist's position and to urge a tolerance of the differences highlighted by her relativism. Since there is no one objective set of moral standards, she will argue, it is sheer arrogance to think that we ever have the right to insist that our moral view, or that of our own society or culture, is right and that someone else's is wrong.[2] According to the moral relativist, moral beliefs are relative to whatever standards a particular society or individual happens to have accepted. And there is, on this view, no objective moral basis for the selection made; no valid exercise of moral reasoning which could **justify** the standards chosen. And the reason is simple: if we were to use moral reasoning, we would have to use the very standards we wanted to justify. But this would be circular, and circular arguments provide no reason to believe their conclusions.

If Moral Relativism is true, then not only does it seem to follow that there is no objective moral truth; it follows that each of the normative theories studied in Part II of this book—utilitarianism, Kantian deontology, etc.—can be nothing more than the articulation of its author's own personal moral beliefs, or those of his society. It further follows that we seem to have no moral basis for choosing among the theories offered, or for putting forward our own moral theory as a reasonable alternative. Moral philosophy, the study of ethical theories and the arguments in their favour, would reduce to a mere **description** of various moral systems or codes and the non-moral rationalizations offered in their favour, with no means available for assessing their validity or truth. Since Moral Relativism presents such a formidable challenge, we would do well to begin with careful consideration of its nature, consequences and validity.

Two Forms of Moral Relativism—Moral Conventionalism and Moral Subjectivism

Moral Relativism is a view which rejects the notion that there is one, universally valid morality which can be discovered by valid moral reasoning. We might define the position as follows.

Moral Relativism   (1) there are no universally valid standards.

(2) the validity of moral standards is dependent on:
    (i) cultural acceptance (**Conventionalism**); or
    (ii) personal choice or commitment (**Subjectivism**).

As the above definition suggests, there are basically two forms of Moral Relativism. According to **Moral Conventionalism**, the validity of moral standards depends on their acceptance within a particular cultural group. **Moral Subjectivism**, on the other hand, asserts that the validity of moral standards depends on their acceptance by an individual (a valid moral principle is one which is valid **for me**). What might lead one to accept either of these views? Though closely related, it is possible to distinguish three different arguments in favour of Moral Relativism.

Three Main Arguments for Moral Relativism

The Diversity Argument

The most commonly cited reason given in favour of Moral Relativism is the undeniable fact of widespread difference of opinion on important moral questions. Some societies have considered slavery to be within the natural order of things, while others have condemned it as a moral abomination. Many individuals view abortion as nothing short of murder, while others condemn attempts to prevent abortions as unacceptable violations of a woman's right to control her own reproductive processes. How, in the light of such vast differences of opinion—which can of course be endlessly multiplied—can it possibly be reasonable to believe in an objective moral truth? How reasonable can it be to believe that there are, in reality, objectively valid moral standards upon which well informed, reasonable people could be expected to agree? If there were such standards, would one not expect to find a good deal more agreement on moral matters than one actually discovers? Perhaps. But as we shall see later, one can go a long way towards acknowledging this lack of agreement on moral matters before one is forced to abandon the thesis that there are some objectively valid moral standards. Even so staunch a defender of objective moral standards as the medieval theologian, St. Thomas Aquinas, is able to provide a good deal of room for moral diversity. But more on this later.

The Demonstrability Argument

A second argument in favour of Moral Relativism seizes on the fact that it is seldom possible to demonstrate, to the satisfaction of all open-minded, reasonable individuals of good will and integrity, that one's moral standards and beliefs are correct. According to defenders of this second argument, the main reason that there is little consensus on moral standards is the absence of an agreed procedure or method of moral reasoning by which individuals can demonstrate to one another the correctness of their moral views. Unlike, say, the natural sciences, where, it is said, there are such agreed procedures, acceptable to the entire scientific community, for demonstrating conclusions, moral reasoning affords no comparable methodology. In contrast with the sciences, one finds within the moral realm a plethora of moral codes, belief systems and theories. These different theories include not only different moral standards, they also prescribe different methods of moral assessment. Some theories are consequentialist, others are deontological. Some of the latter eschew appeal to consequences entirely, others believe only that more than consequences can be relevant. Some theories consider moral values to be central to moral life; others assert that values are secondary and dependent on judgments of obligation. In the light of such widespread disagreements, it would be foolish to believe that there is anything like a method of moral demonstration which comes even close to emulating the methods of the natural sciences. But without the possibility of demonstration, moral views can be nothing more than matters of opinion (Moral Subjectivism). At best, they must be relativised to a particular society or culture (Moral Conventionalism).

The Divine Authority Argument

Some Moral Relativists base their rejection of universally valid moral standards on their rejection of God. These relativists conceive of morality as identical with, or at the very least closely analogous with, a set of commands or directives. If the fundamental question of morality is "How shall I live my life?" the answer, they say, would be a directive or command of the form "Do this!" Since it is in the very nature of a command that it must issue from a person (e.g., a general or the Department Chairperson) or an authoritative group of persons (e.g., Parliament or Congress) it follows that there must be a commander of moral standards. Now if, as the moral objectivist asserts, moral standards truly are universally valid for all times, places and peoples, the only plausible commander would seem to be God, who is thought (by those who believe in his existence) to possess divine authority over the universe. God as moral commander not only determines which standards are universally valid, he/she also imbues them with their binding authority. But if there is no such being, then there can be no universally valid moral standards—and we are left trying to find a person or persons whose "commands" determine which moral standards are valid. We have, the moral relativist says, no better place to look than to the individual (Subjectivism) or his society or culture (Moral Conventionalism). The authority of God is supplanted by the authority of the individual or her community.

The preceding three arguments are often thought to provide a sound basis for Moral Relativism. Whether, in the end, the arguments provide a persuasive case is a question which cannot be decided till we delve more deeply into the theoretical underpinnings of the theory and its rivals. There is reason for skepticism, however, because there are additional key features of moral life for which Moral Relativism does not appear to provide a wholly satisfactory philosophical account. Some of the alleged consequences of Relativism are taken by many to be an adequate basis for rejecting the theory out of hand. As will become clear, however, many of the commonly supposed consequences of Relativism may not in fact follow at all.

Alleged Consequences of Moral Conventionalism

A Basis for Moral Criticism?

The most oft cited objection to Moral Conventionalism is that we seem barred from saying that the moral standards of another culture are wrong, or morally inferior to those of our own culture. This is because there are no objective, culturally neutral moral standards with which we could compare the practices of another culture with those of our own and deem them morally deficient or wanting in some way. All we have are our standards which apply to our culture; and all they have are their standards which apply to their culture. And these are, **by definition**, morally correct (for the relevant parties). Consider the many slave societies which have existed over the centuries, including the Ancient Greek culture of the philosopher Aristotle who accepted the moral propriety of this practice. Slavery is usually premised on the belief that some groups of individuals are morally less worthy than others, and that the lesser groups are naturally suited to serve the interests of the superior group who excel in things like intelligence, the capacity to exercise virtue, and so on. Most of us in modern Western societies would like to say that these beliefs, and the standards and practices resting upon them, are terribly wrong. But if Conventionalism is correct, we seem barred from saying this. Or so it is said.

Room for the Moral Reformer?

For much the same reasons the position of the moral reformer or critic is commonly thought to be incoherent if Moral Conventionalism is true. Suppose the culture whose moral practices I wish to criticize are not someone else's but **mine**. Suppose that I am the one who lives in a society whose conventional moral practices clearly incorporate the institution of slavery and that I reject this terrible view completely. I sincerely believe slavery to be morally wrong. In fact, I believe it to be an abomination which must at all costs be eradicated from all civilized societies. Suppose now that I make the following claim to anyone who will listen: "Slavery is morally wrong." If Moral Conventionalism is true, then, prima facie, my claim is necessarily incorrect or false, as anyone who cared to do so could easily demonstrate to me. Since slavery is, as a matter of fact, morally sanctioned by the conventional standards of my society, it appears to follow from Moral Conventionalism that my critical claim **cannot be right**. At best I can be interpreted as saying—on some ground other than morality—that slavery **should not** be moral. Perhaps I could argue, on purely **prudential** grounds, that our collective self-interest suggests that we should ban slavery because it eventually leads to serious social instability. Or perhaps I could argue, on strictly **economic** grounds, that slavery is an inefficient system of production better replaced by a fully open, free-market system in which former slaves are economically motivated to contribute productively to the economy. All of these are possible reasons for criticizing the practice of slavery as it is found within my society. But none serves as a **moral** reason. If Moral Conventionalism is true, it would seem that I cannot intelligently deny that slavery is, as a matter of fact, a morally justified practice. I seem left with no intelligible space in which to criticize my culture's practices on moral grounds.

Failure to provide intelligible space for the moral reformer is a serious shortcoming of any theory of morality. A moral reformer wants to say, not that certain moral standards should no longer be moral, but that they are **not moral standards at all**, despite their widespread acceptance. And Moral Conventionalism seems, prima facie, to bar her from saying this. The problem can perhaps best be viewed by contrasting morality with law. Unlike morality, law is clearly, at root, a matter of convention—what is legal within a community is, in the end, a matter of what is accepted as legal within that community. If a rule meets the conditions of legality accepted within a society—e.g., it has been duly passed by the

legislature and does not violate relevant constitutional principles — then it **is** a legally valid rule for that society. One who
disagrees with the rule can argue that it should not be a legal
rule, perhaps because it violates fundamental moral principles, or because it stifles economic expansion, but she cannot
argue that it is not a valid legal rule. Moral Conventionalism
appears to say the same thing about moral standards — that
their acceptance within a culture determines their validity.
But law and morality seem importantly different in this respect. Whether a rule, practice or principle is morally correct
seems to be a function of whether it is supported by **good
reasons** of a moral kind, whether it can be backed up by
sound moral reasoning. It is not a function of whether, as a
matter of contingent social fact, it happens to be **accepted
as moral** by a group of people whose beliefs, values, practices, and so on, define a culture. So Moral Conventionalism
is on shaky ground. It seems to make morality too much like
law.

Which Culture?

So far our discussion of Moral Conventionalism has assumed
that we can always identify a culture in relation to which
moral standards are to be identified and understood. But this
assumption is highly questionable. The fact of the matter is
that we all live within a multiplicity of cultures. But if this is
the case, and if Conventionalism is correct, it seems to follow
that a person wishing to answer the fundamental question of
morality, "How shall I live my life?" may be left with many
different answers — and no means of choosing amongst them.
This, it might be argued, is sufficient reason to reject Moral
Conventionalism and look for an alternative theory.

Three :: *It's All Just Relative—Or Is It?*

The notion of a "culture" is a notoriously difficult notion to define, but however one defines it, there is little doubt that we all live in different cultures simultaneously. A person can be an American, a Texan, a Christian, a Roman Catholic, an Irish-American, a citizen of Galveston, a member of the local Elk Lodge, a member of a "National Society for the Promotion of Family Values," an alumnus of the local high school, a member of a baseball team, a member of a corporation, and so on. Each of these "cultures" is defined, in part, by shared values, principles, beliefs, practices, and perhaps a shared identity and history. But however these cultures are understood, it is clear that they can differ dramatically from one another in their expectations of individual members. As a member of the local Elk Lodge Tom might be committed to accepting the practice of raising money through special "casino nights"; as a member of the National Society for the Promotion of Family Values he might be committed to condemning this practice as pandering to the baser elements of human character. As a practising Roman Catholic Mary might be required to condemn abortion; as a judge practising within the American legal community she might be under moral obligation to apply the law, even when this requires her to support the rights of women to therapeutic abortions. If moral right and wrong are relative to culture, Tom and Mary seem to face serious dilemmas. Without a reason to prefer the requirement of one of their "cultures" over the other, they are left with no answer to the question whether casino nights are morally permissible or whether abortion is morally wrong. And there is no reason, within the theory of Moral Conventionalism, to support a preference for one culture over the other.

Alleged Consequences of Subjectivism[3]

The Possibility of Genuine Moral Disagreement

Perhaps the most telling difficulty with Subjectivism is that it appears to exclude the possibility of genuine, substantive, moral **disagreement**.[4] Subjectivism asserts that all my moral judgments are relative to whatever choice of moral standards I happen to make. What is morally right **for me** depends on the standards to which I subscribe. What is morally right **for you** depends on the standards to which you happen to subscribe.[5] Suppose that I believe that abortion is morally wrong under all conditions, while you believe that abortion is morally permissible, at least till the point where the fetus is viable, that is, able to survive independently of the woman who carries it. My belief is based on my acceptance of the moral principle that human life is sacred in both its actual and potential forms. Your belief is based on your acceptance of a very strong principle of autonomy which requires unfettered liberty, on the part of women, to make and act upon decisions involving their own reproductive capacities.

Notice an important consequence of this scenario if Subjectivism is true. Despite the appearance of conflict in our moral judgments, there may, in fact, be no moral disagreement between us at all! It is possible that each of us has, in fact, judged correctly, has got things right. The reason for this odd consequence lies in the very nature of Subjectivism: if correct moral judgments are always relative to the moral standards of the individual making the judgments, then so long as I correctly apply my standards, and you yours, we are both right, despite the fact that we **appear** to disagree. The reason there is no genuine dispute between us is similar to the reason we were barred from judging our culture's morality superior to slave cultures: there are no "inter-subjective" or "objectively valid" principles to which we can appeal in assessing our relative positions. Consequently we cannot intelligently view ourselves as in dispute with one another **about what the correct principles require,** nor can we appeal to any standards to resolve our differences. Each of us is correct, for his part alone. And this is all one seems able to say, if Subjectivism is true, about apparently conflicting moral judgments.

But this cannot be right. Whatever else might be true of morality, it is clearly a practice whose very nature is to guide us in determining what to do—to help us in determining which courses of action we should be pursuing and why. By its very nature morality is a means of helping to resolve disputes among people and of answering fundamental questions about how they should lead their lives. Subjectivism, which effectively says that the right moral standards are whatever ones I happen to accept, seems to rob morality of its critical, action-guiding character.

Moral Reasoning and Argument?

A closely related difficulty for Subjectivism—one which it again shares with Conventionalism—is the diminished role it appears to provide for moral **reasoning** and **argumentation.** Not only do there appear to be no genuine, inter-subjective moral disputes if Moral Subjectivism is true, but there seems to be no substantive basis for us to reason and argue with each other—or with ourselves—about which standards are morally better. This is because, once again, what is morally right is always a function of my choices, i.e., is determined by whatever moral standards I happen to choose. I can prefer one set of standards because, e.g., following them will serve my own prudential interests, or because they are the ones upon which I was raised and with which I am most comfortable. But these are not moral reasons. If Subjectivism is true, moral reflection seems to provide no reason to prefer one set of standards over another. It cannot give me any basis for trying to persuade you rationally (i.e., on the basis of good reasons) that my standards are better, morally speaking, than yours.

Relativism: A Partial Defence and Lessons to Be Learned

So what are we to say of Moral Relativism? If the alleged consequences sketched above are indeed attributable to the theory, then we seem to have powerful reasons for rejecting it. Any theoretical account of morality which excludes the very possibility of genuine moral argument and critique just has to be wrong, despite the support provided by the Diversity Argument, the Demonstrability Argument and the Divine Authority Argument. But are moral argument and critique truly impossible on the relativist account? The answer is a qualified "No." Moral Relativism is in fact quite compatible with these features of morality because even if culture or subjective choice provide us with our moral standards, moral reasoning may still be necessary in deciding at least three different kinds of questions which invariably crop up in any moral dispute: **factual questions, application questions** and **questions of consistency**.[6] Let's consider each of these in turn.

Factual Questions

Within all spheres of inquiry, whether theoretical or practical, it is always essential to get one's facts straight. Whatever reasons we might have for believing a proposition, or for choosing some particular course of conduct or appraising some object as good or bad, our reasons are not good ones if they rest on shaky factual ground. A scientific theory of planetary motion is inadequate if it rests on dubious factual claims about the behaviour of the planets. Theories which rested on the highly plausible claim that the plants travel round the Sun in circular orbits had to be rejected once the observations of astronomers like Johannes Kepler and Tycho Brahe revealed that the orbits were in fact elliptical. In this case, a theoretical dispute in science turned, largely, on getting the facts straight. The same holds true when it comes to morality. What appears to be a **substantive moral** dispute, a "difference of principle" perhaps, often turns out to rest on nothing more than a difference of opinion on non-moral facts. Affirmative action programs[7] have long given rise to tremendous moral controversy. But often these controversies are traceable to differences in factual belief. Are the members of the minority group truly disadvantaged in their quest for educational and employment opportunities? Or are the disadvantages undoubtedly suffered by their mothers and fathers now a thing of the past? Will showing preference to minority candidates in fact provide them with the desired advantage, or will such factors as resentment, and the widespread belief that the preferred candidates are not up to the job, strip the preferred candidates of any real advantage? Will such factors actually result in **disadvantage** for many minority candidates whose superior qualifications for the positions gained will always be questioned? These are all largely factual questions upon which defenders and opponents of affirmative action often disagree.

These differences in **factual** belief can lead to very different **moral** beliefs regarding the moral propriety of affirmative action programs. Those who see continued, serious disadvantage may well believe that affirmative action is morally necessary despite its acknowledged costs. Others who believe that serious disadvantage is a thing of the past, may well believe that affirmative action is morally questionable because it in fact does more harm than good to the intended beneficiaries. This is not to say, of course, that all disputes surrounding affirmative action reduce, in the end, to factual disputes. One who accepts that more harm than good might result from affirmative action programs may yet support these programs on grounds of justice. In the view of many justice requires that a debt be paid, even if, in the end, the consequences of doing so are, for all those affected, worse than the consequences of not doing so. In other words, one who agrees with an opponent of affirmative action on the consequences of such a practice may yet support it for deontological reasons. It is the right thing to do, she will say, even though better overall consequences would result from its elimination. So even though we must realize that much of what passes for substantive moral argumentation is, in reality, factual dispute, we must be careful not to overstate the case.

So how does this all bear on the plausibility of Moral Relativism? As should now be clear, even if Moral Relativism were true there would still be considerable space for moral argument and critique. Although we have yet to see how, on either form of relativism, one could be in substantive moral dispute about the validity of moral standards which are in fact accepted by the relevant person or culture, it remains quite possible to be in dispute about the factual beliefs upon which that acceptance is based. It is (and was) quite possible to criticize slave-owning societies by demonstrating that the factual beliefs upon which their practices rest are completely false. And this is true of moral reformers both within and external to such societies. Among the relevant false beliefs was the conviction that a particular race of individuals was lacking in reason, or in the capacity to govern itself with a minimal level of prudence. Such beliefs, upon which many slave societies have been based, were all completely false. And demonstrating their falsity was one important step towards moral reform.

Application Questions

Not only is reasoning necessary to establish, or question, the factual basis of moral stances, it is equally necessary in deciding how to apply moral standards to particular situations. Suppose that you have adopted a principle which says that human life is sacred and must **always** be preserved. Now imagine that Subjectivism is the correct theory about the status of morality and moral judgments.[8] It seems to follow that no one can argue with you, on moral grounds, that your sanctity principle is wrong.[9] Of equal importance is the fact that you have no way of determining, for yourself, that this principle is objectively the morally right one for you to adopt. Again, this is because moral reasons are relative to the choice of standards you happen to make, including your choice of moral principles. So there seem to be, for you, no legitimate **moral** questions once you have adopted your principle, no exercise in moral reasoning through which you must go to justify the moral choices you are now in a position to make. But this appearance is illusory. You may yet be left with very serious, and more often than not immensely difficult, questions concerning the requirements of your principle. This is because moral standards must invariably be **applied** and **interpreted**, and for this a kind of moral reasoning is required.

Consider the following case where very difficult application questions arise. Suppose you are a surrogate decision maker, charged with deciding what should be done in the case of a dear friend, Jeff, who has been in a serious accident. As a result of the head trauma experienced in the accident, Jeff is in a "persistent vegetative state." In other words, he has no hope of ever regaining any form of consciousness. He will never again be aware of anything, including his own existence. Let's further assume that there is no basis for knowing what Jeff might have wanted done in the circumstances, and that there is no one else, e.g., a family friend, who could be consulted. The decision is entirely yours. And recall that you have accepted the Sanctity of Life principle. Does this mean that you now know what to do? Certainly not. You are faced with a difficult question concerning the application of your principle. Does your Sanctity of Life principle apply in this particular case? Does it apply in the case of an accident victim in a persistent vegetative state who has no hope of ever regaining all those mental capacities which make us distinctly human? Must he be kept "alive" in such circumstances? Or has the "life" of one in such a state already ended? Is it perhaps true that Jeff, the person, is no longer there, that what remains is nothing more than a biological organism? If so, then perhaps the Sanctity of Life principle no longer applies to him? In order to answer these immensely difficult application questions, you will need to reason about the conditions under which a "human life" can be said to exist. Does it require some measure of consciousness, some capacity to sense the world and engage in practical reasoning? Does it require the ability to communicate, at some minimal level at least, with other human persons?

It is crucial to notice that questions such as these can never be answered in a purely scientific manner. In determining whether an individual in a persistent vegetative state still possesses "human life" you are asking whether such a person, in this case Jeff, still possesses whatever properties and capacities one is deeming worthy of protection and promotion according to your principle. But deciding which capacities and properties are **worthy** of protection and promotion seems clearly to involve a **judgment of moral value**. In saying that a human life is sacred because, and to the extent that, it possesses such things as the capacity to reason and to enter into social relationships you are ascribing moral value to the possession of these properties. In short, you cannot apply your moral principle without exercising what appears to be straightforward moral argumentation.

True enough, it might be replied. But all this shows is that in applying one subjectively chosen moral standard (e.g., the Sanctity Principle) to a new situation, one might have to appeal to some other subjectively chosen standard (e.g., the moral value of sentience, etc.). But the latter has no more claim to being objectively valid than the former—its validity depends on our ultimate choices (Subjectivism) or those of our culture (Conventionalism). And so there remains, for the Relativist, no space for substantive argument about, and critique of, our fundamental moral commitments. This is a point which may in the end have to be acknowledged. However, the aim of the preceding paragraph was not to force the Relativist to acknowledge that there are objectively valid moral standards. The aim was only to answer the charge that Moral Relativism must be rejected on the ground that it is incompatible with substantive moral argument and reasoning. As Jeff's case reveals, once a standard has been (subjectively or culturally) chosen, much often needs to be done in the way of moral reasoning because application questions will inevitably arise, and these can often be answered only by way of moral reasoning.

Consistency Questions

So reasoning is involved when we try to apply our moral standards to new, or freshly reconsidered, situations—and this is true even if Moral Relativism is valid. Reasoning is also required in countless situations in which (a) accepted moral standards appear to conflict with one another; or (b) when an accepted standard seems to require conduct which is deemed for some other reason to be unacceptable. In both cases, reasoning helps to establish, and perhaps evaluate, the **implications** of the relevant standards—implications which must either be accepted or rejected and which may call for a revision of previously accepted standards. In the first instance, (a), reason reveals one particular kind of implication: one adopted standard requires conduct rejected by a competing adopted standard. In the second case, (b), it reveals an implication I may not, for some other reason, find acceptable. Recall Hare's point that I must be willing to accept the **universal** application of whatever principle I act upon.[10] And this includes, of course, all those actual or hypothetical applications where I am on the losing end of someone else's conduct. Unless I am willing to accept all these implications, then logical consistency bars me from accepting and acting on my principle. Perhaps, upon reflecting on these matters, it becomes clear to me that my principle requires far too much in the way of self-sacrifice. If so, then logical consistency and

moral integrity require that I abandon or modify my principle.

Consider a situation involving the kind of conflict described in (a) above. I have adopted two principles whose
requirements conflict. Suppose I have accepted both the
principle that I ought always to tell the truth, **T**, and the
principle that I ought always to avoid conduct which results
in serious harm to my friends, **H**. It takes little imagination
to think up scenarios in which **T** and **H** provide conflicting advice. Suppose a suicidal friend shows up at my front
door asking where I have hid his hand gun. What am I to do
if I am a subjectivist? My subjectively chosen truth-telling
principle, **T**, tells me that I ought to reveal the whereabouts
of the gun. My subjectively chosen harm principle, **H**, tells
me that I ought **not** to reveal the whereabouts of the gun.
If I am to resolve the conflict between my principles, I am
going to have to modify at least one of them to provide for
exceptions. Perhaps I should modify **T** in order to allow for
an exception involving serious harm to my friends. But is this
the right compromise? Would I be willing to accept that the
gun should be handed over if the one who requests it is not
my friend? But why should that be relevant? Am I willing to
accept a principle according to which I must avoid harming
my friends, but am free to harm seriously those who are not
my friends? What reason could possibly be given for such a
distinction? None, it would seem; the distinction seems, from
a moral point of view, to be arbitrary. So perhaps my principle should be that I should always tell the truth unless great
harm would result to **anyone at all**, including those who are
not my friends.

The compromise sketched in the preceding paragraph is
not, of course, the only one open to me. Alternatively, I might
modify **H** instead of **T**. Maybe I should avoid conduct which

results in serious harm to others (not just my friends) **unless that conduct is required by some other principle** like **T**, the principle that one ought always to tell the truth. This is a strong deontological position to which Kant subscribed. It seems open to me as well, so long as I am willing to live with its implications. By allowing me in this way to draw out the implications of my subjectively chosen principles, reason can reveal the nature of the various choices open to me. What it cannot do, if Subjectivism is true, is make the choice for me. If Subjectivism is true, there may be no moral reason to prefer one way of reconciling my conflicting principles over another. And the same can be said of Moral Conventionalism.

Three Arguments for Moral Relativism: A Preliminary Response

Earlier we sketched three arguments often given in favour of Moral Relativism. We are now in a much better position to assess their merits and to see why they have only limited force.

The Diversity Argument

The most powerful argument in favour of Moral Relativism is no doubt the Diversity Argument. If, as seems all too apparent, there is widespread disagreement on moral questions, is it not foolish to believe that there is an objective moral truth, that there are objectively valid, universal moral standards which determine right answers to moral questions? Perhaps. But consider the following points. **First,** from the fact that there is widespread disagreement on a question it fails to follow that it has no answer. Historians often disagree profoundly on what occurred centuries ago. But few are willing

86

to infer from this that there are no historical truths. **Second**, moral reasoning is very complex and difficult. Perhaps we have yet to reach the stage where we understand fully the complex dimensions of many moral issues. Maybe we are still trying to figure things out. But there is no denying that we have made progress over the years. As noted on several occasions above, slavery was once believed to be a morally acceptable practice. It is now almost universally condemned as the moral abomination it surely is. I take this to be significant progress. Can we not hope for similar increases in moral enlightenment in the future? **Third**, many moral disputes rest on ignorance of the facts. Returning to our slavery example, acceptance of this practice rested on false factual beliefs about the intellectual and non-cognitive capacities of those deemed unworthy of full moral status. Science proved these beliefs to be groundless, thus giving force to movements in favour of abolition. Might not the same be true of disputes surrounding things like the use of human embryos for stem cell extraction, the effects of affirmative action programs, or the existence of factory farms? Even if agreement on the relevant scientific facts fails to yield full moral consensus, a good deal of moral disagreement can nonetheless be explained by differences in factual beliefs.

Finally, we come to an important **fourth** point. The extent to which the world's populations accept, or have accepted, different moral standards may be seriously overstated by defenders of Moral Relativism. As we will see more fully when we explore the details of St. Thomas Aquinas' natural law theory of morality, it is quite possible that universally valid moral principles and values are to some degree **indeterminate** and must be fleshed out or interpreted in light of differing social and environmental circumstances. One and the same principle might well yield different results in different situations. Consider, again, the sanctity of human life principle. It seems quite likely that many societies in which medical science is less advanced than ours will interpret this principle as requiring that **all possible efforts** be made to save the lives of dying patients, regardless of the costs, both personal and monetary. This was arguably our society 100 years ago. When medical science was in its infancy, it was possible to read the sanctity of life principle as demanding, with the respect to saving the lives of dying patients, that "whatever **ought** to be done" be treated as equivalent to "whatever **can** be done." But our situation today is very different. We are able to keep patients, including those like Jeff who are in a persistent vegetative state, alive for very long periods of time. We are able to do this but only at great social and economic costs. These costs include the use — some would say "squandering" — of scarce resources which might otherwise have gone to help patients with different medical conditions. It is arguable that in this more advanced world of medical technologies the sanctity of life principle just cannot be interpreted as requiring the equivalence of "whatever ought to be done" with "whatever can be done." Different circumstances yield different interpretations or applications — of one and the same principle. Generalizing from this example, the possibility emerges that there is much more agreement on basic moral standards than initially meets the eye. What the Moral Relativist takes to be differences in moral standards may, in many instances, reduce to differences in the interpretation of the very same moral standards.

The Demonstrability Argument

The absence of agreed procedures for demonstrating moral conclusions is often taken to be an argument in favour of

Moral Relativism. Morality, it is claimed, lacks the agreement on methods and procedures that one finds in the natural sciences. As a result moral conclusions cannot be demonstrated and are just "matters of opinion." This popular argument is no more persuasive than the Diversity Argument. **First**, it rests on a highly dubious assumption: that the objectivity of a practice requires agreed methods of demonstration which, when applied properly, always yield results upon which fully informed participants would be forced to agree (on pain of being deemed irrational). This assumption is, at best, questionable. Many social practices, e.g., law, literary criticism and history, thrive in the absence of such agreed methods and results. Take historical explanation. There are few agreed standards of theory construction and evaluation upon which all historians agree. And for many historical events or trends, there are no historical explanations upon which all historians will ultimately agree. Yet virtually no one denies that there is (at least normally) a "truth of the matter" which historians seek to discover and explain. Historians believe that they are seeking the truth, and are able, in intelligent ways, to develop, evaluate and critique historical explanations. All this despite the fact that they are seldom able to demonstrate their conclusions to the complete satisfaction of everyone. Why should the same not apply to the ethical theorist and his accounts of the nature and status of morality and moral practices? Unless we wish to condemn all of these practices as wholly misguided, we must reject the Demonstrability Argument. It seems questionable at best. There is no reason, therefore, to conclude from the absence of agreement on clear-cut methods of demonstration that everything is up for grabs, that there is no moral truth.

A **second**, equally important point against the Demonstrability Argument is that the comparison with the natural sciences unjustifiably flatters the latter. The advantage held by the supposedly rigorous methodology of science over the comparatively undisciplined methods of moral reasoning rests upon an exaggerated contrast between the two. The fact of the matter is that the history of science is replete with controversy about the most fundamental of matters. There has been deep controversy about how to go about testing hypotheses, as well as disputes about substantive matters. Examples of the latter include widespread controversies about the nature of light (is it composed of particles or waves?) and about whether space is a vacuum or is filled with a largely imperceptible "ether." Then there are all the controversies about whether, and to the extent to which, science can be "value free." Scientists not only disagree about scientific facts and theories, they often disagree on what methods are to be employed in developing, defending and evaluating their accounts. For example, scientific differences sometimes turn on disputes over the reliability of a certain apparatus — e.g., a telescope or microscope — in establishing evidence. Other times, differences will hinge on the validity of certain mathematical models used in understanding natural phenomena. Science is not the absolutely rigorous machine many suppose. Despite its many controversies, however, few people are willing to condemn science as wholly subjective or relative. So why should we, on these very same grounds, condemn morality and ethical theory as matters of mere opinion?

One final point. As we saw above when we explored the extent to which even Moral Relativism can accommodate moral argumentation and substantive moral disagreement, there is a good deal that we can all agree on in developing, defending and evaluating moral theories. All of us would agree that we must be sure to get our facts straight, ensure that our principles are consistent, and be willing to accept the implications of our universalized moral judgments. There may well be much more agreement on moral methodology than initially meets the eye.

The Divine Authority Argument

What does one say to the Moral Relativist who offers the following argument?

> If God is dead—i.e., if there is in fact no God whose commands could constitute a universally binding set of moral laws—then there can be no universal morality. Without a divine commander whose commands apply universally, there can be no universal moral law. And if no universal moral law is possible, then moral standards must be the "commands," not of God, but of one's society or culture.

It is not possible to provide a satisfactory answer to this argument without examining in some detail the **Divine Command Theory** of morality considered in the next chapter. Suffice it to say, at this point, that the argument may well rest on a completely false and misleading picture of morality. Moral standards cannot be identified with the commands of anyone, **including God**. Rather, they are standards which are defensible in light of the reasons which support them. If God commands us to behave in certain ways which we take to be constitutive of the moral life, this has to be because he recognizes that this is what morality requires. It must be because he recognizes good moral reasons for commanding the way that he does. But if this is so, then his commands cannot **establish** the requirements of morality. At best they can reflect what is already moral, independently of his commands. Since moral standards are wrongly thought of as the commands of God, we need not conclude, from the absence of a divine commander, that there are no universally binding moral standards. These important points will be further fleshed out and defended in the next chapter.

The Verdict?

So what, in the end, are we to say about Moral Relativism? Perhaps the first thing we must do is stress once again that its refutation (or demonstration) is no simple matter. It is not enough to point out that Relativism is incapable of providing conceptual space for moral argument and critique because, as we have seen, it is quite capable of doing just that. Moral questions often turn on factual disputes, on questions of application or interpretation, and on arguments of consistency. And this is true whether or not moral standards are ultimately relative to person or culture. So the main arguments **against** Moral Relativism have limited force. But it is equally important to appreciate the difficulty in finding conclusive support **for** Relativism. The three arguments offered in its favour, the Diversity Argument, the Demonstrability Argument, and the Divine Authority Argument, all rest on shaky philosophical ground.

So we seem to have some reason for thinking that Relativism could be true, and some reason for thinking that it may be false. A final verdict on the truth of Moral Relativism is impossible without considerably more analysis than is possible in this book. But enough has been said, I hope, to undermine the seemingly obvious (to some) point that when it comes to morality, "everything is relative" or "just a matter of opinion." And enough has been said, I hope, to undermine the equally obvious (to some) point that Moral Relativism is a naive theory which finds no room for things like genuine moral disagreement and the presence of moral reformers. The fact of the matter is that the Relativist **is** able to furnish a reasonably cogent account of these phenomena. In the end, the verdict on Moral Relativism may rest on the plausibility of an alternative account of morality which purports to furnish a universally valid, objective basis for morality. If such a theory can be developed, then we will perhaps have in its articulation the best possible argument against Moral Relativism. One such theory attempts to establish an objective ground for moral standards in God's natural law or in his commands. It is to this theory that we now turn.

Notes

1. For ease of expression we will continue to use the phrase "moral standard" to refer to moral principles, rules, values, practices, and so on. For example, when we say that, in the view of the moral conventionalist, the validity of moral standards is relative to a culture, we should be understood to say that this is true of some set or mixture of principles, rules, values and practices.

2. Whether Moral Relativism provides the best case for rejecting moral imperialism is, at best, questionable. If there is no basis for discovering objective moral truth, then there is nothing to prevent a society or person from adopting a moral code which licences moral imperialism.

3. As will be clear, most of the alleged difficulties associated with Subjectivism apply equally to Conventionalism. We will concern ourselves here with cognitive versions of Subjectivism which claim that moral judgments assert propositions which we put forward as true, and are justified by the moral standards to which we personally subscribe. Closely related, though distinguishable, are non-cognitivist forms of Subjectivism which say that moral judgments do not assert propositions at all. On non-cognitivist theories like emotivism, see the preceding chapter.

4. This difficulty seems applicable to Emotivism as well, especially the crude form espoused by Ayer. See preceding chapter.

5. Again, Moral Conventionalism has a similar consequence. It would appear that **genuine** moral disagreement can no more exist between different cultures than it can between different individuals.

6. These are questions which apply regardless of whether relativism is true or not. Moral reasoning, on any plausible ethical theory, including emotivism, natural law theory, social contract theory, the ethics of care, and so on, involves in some way these three kinds of questions.

7. These are programs in which members of a minority group are given preference over those of a majority group when it comes to things like employment and educational opportunities.

8. Analogous points can be made if we substitute Moral Conventionalism.

9. As we will see shortly, this is not quite true. It could be shown, for example, that my principle is inconsistent with some other principle I do not wish to reject or modify. If so, then it is possible to show me that I **must** reject the sanctity of life principle.

10. See Chapter 2 above for a discussion of Hare's universal prescriptivism. This feature of moral judgments—that we must be willing to universalize our judgment to cover all situations just like ours—will be explored further in Chapter 7.

Four
Morality and Religion: Divine Command Theory and Natural Law

An Objective Basis for Morality?

Those who seek an objective basis for morality often look to religion or theology. Linking moral standards to God's authority appears to provide not only a means of grounding morality in something other than subjective or cultural choice, it seems to provide an explanation of why we should follow the dictates of morality. In this chapter we will consider two very different ways of linking morality with religion and theology. First we will consider the Divine Command theory, discussed by Plato in his dialogue the *Euthyphro* and later by Leibniz in his *Discourse on Metaphysics*. Then we will turn to an account of Natural Law theory, as outlined and defended by St. Thomas Aquinas in his monumental work, the *Summa Theologica*.[1]

Divine Command Theory

According to Divine Command theory the true standard of moral right and wrong lies in the will of God. More specifically, moral standards are nothing more and nothing less than the **commands** of God which instruct us in how we are to behave. Why should we refrain from telling lies? Because God has commanded that we tell the truth. Why should we avoid harming other people? Because God has commanded us to do so. Why do we have a moral right to make our own decisions regarding medical treatment? Because God has commanded others to respect our claim-right to the exercise of this power, or He has commanded others to observe a rule or principle from which it follows that we have that right and that they have the corresponding obligation.

Two Versions of Divine Command Theory

Defenders of Divine Command theory can make one of two very different assertions. First, the theory can be understood as making a claim about the **grounds** for our moral judgments. This **Moral Ground** version of Divine Command theory says that the grounds for our moral claims lie in God's will or commands. If X is morally right, this is **because** God has commanded that we do X. In other words, the **reason** why we should do X is the sheer fact that God commanded us to do X. The **reason** why principle P is a valid moral standard is that God has commanded P.

   In addition to the Moral Ground version of Divine Command theory, there is a second theory, easily confused with the first.[2] On this particular version, God does indeed always command us to do the morally right thing. But his commanding us to do X is not what **makes** X the morally right thing to do. In other words, X is not morally right **because** God commanded X. Rather, God commands us to do X **because it is the morally right thing to do**. Being a supremely perfect being, with unlimited knowledge and benevolence, God knows the true standards of morality and lets us know what these are. Let's call this version of the Divine Command theory the **Divine Index** version. According to this particular form of the theory, God's command is an infallible guide or index to what is, on grounds wholly independent of his command, morally right and wrong. His command does not, however, as it does on the Moral Ground version of Divine Command Theory, **establish** what is right or wrong. The Divine Index theory is consistent with a wide range of different normative moral theories. Among the standards God might instruct us to observe, for example, are the principle of utility or Kant's Categorical Imperative.

The Moral Ground Version

The early modern philosopher Leibniz provides us with a succinct introduction to the pitfalls of the Moral Ground version of the Divine Command theory. In discussing why God chose to create this, the best of all possible worlds, Leibniz entertains the possibility that the "principles of perfection" which governed God's choice were those decreed or commanded by God himself.[3] Those attracted by this particular theory are motivated largely by the wish to avoid diminishing God's power and freedom. Were his choices governed or constrained by something other than his own will, it seems to follow that God could not possibly be omnipotent. A God whose choices are **constrained** by anything at all—including the requirement that he observe moral principles—cannot possibly be an all powerful God, free to act in any way he sees fit. One way round this dilemma seems to be to assert that it is God himself who determines which moral principles are valid. Hence his decisions are ultimately determined by nothing but his own choices. He remains all-powerful and free.

So the wish to maintain God's infinite power is largely behind the Moral Grounds Version of the Divine Command theory. But as Leibniz easily shows, it is highly questionable whether the theory succeeds in achieving the objectives of its proponents. It has troublesome implications which its defenders would be loathe to accept.

> Thus I am far removed from the opinion of those who maintain that there are no rules of goodness and perfection in the nature of things ... and who say that the works of God are good solely from the formal reason that God has made them. For, if this were so, God, knowing that he is their author, would not have had to consider them afterwards and find them good, as is testified by the Sacred Scriptures ... I confess that the contrary opinion seems to me extremely dangerous and very near to the opinion of the recent innovators who hold that the beauty of the universe and the goodness we attribute to the works of God are but the chimeras of those who conceive of God in terms of themselves. Thus, in saying that things are not good by virtue of any rule of goodness but solely by virtue of the will of God, it seems to me that we unknowingly destroy all of God's love and all of his glory. For why praise him for what he has done if he would be equally praiseworthy in doing the exact contrary.[4]

According to Leibniz, if God's choice **determines** the standards of right and wrong, then we have no basis upon which to praise God for the choices he makes. We can't praise God for making the right choices if there are no independent standards according to which we can assess those choices (and the actions which follow from them) and determine that they match those standards perfectly. Nor can we assess God's character as being morally superior. All we end up saying, in praising God for always making the right choices, is that God's choices are in accordance with the choices he makes. All we end up saying, in praising God's supremely moral character, is that his character, as revealed in the choices he makes, is in accordance with those choices. And these are hardly adequate bases for praising someone.

Yet another troubling implication of the Moral Grounds version of Divine Command theory is this: if there are no objectively right standards to which God necessarily adheres in commanding what He does—if, that is, moral standards are simply a function of God's naked will—then his commands become wholly **arbitrary**. Whatever God commands us to do must be morally right. Since there is no moral reason for choosing one way rather than another, God could just as easily have commanded us to torture or kill one another just for the fun of it, as he could have chosen to prohibit these activities. Had he done so, then torturing and killing would be the right thing to do. Notice that it is no use to reply that God could never command such things because of his perfect goodness and because these things are morally wrong. And the reason is simple: there **are no standards of perfect goodness** on this theory independent of what God happens to choose, which could be used to support the claim that a perfectly moral God could not possibly command such things. If God commanded torture, then, on the

Moral Ground version of Divine Command theory, such an action would have to be moral—because, after all, God did command it. We must always bear in mind what this particular version of the theory tells us: that the validity of a moral standard is **determined** by nothing more and nothing less than God's naked command. So if God were to command us to murder each other with impunity, that would have to be the right thing for us to do. But most people are unwilling to accept this implication.

In light of Leibniz's objections we are led to conclude that the Moral Ground version of the Divine Command theory gets things backwards.[5] Moral standards are not valid because God commanded them. Rather, whatever standards God might command us to observe, he does so because those particular standards are valid moral standards. If God's commands are to be used as a measure of right and wrong, then they can only serve as a guide or index to objectively correct standards of morality whose validity lies in something other than God's will. This leads to the second type of Divine Command theory, the Moral Index version.

The Moral Index Version of the Divine Command Theory

According to the Moral Index version of Divine Command theory, God's word does not determine valid moral standards. Rather it serves as a reliable guide to what those standards are. And such a guide would, of course, be a very good thing to have. If we knew with some measure of certainty what God has commanded us to do, then we would know what morally we ought to do. We might not understand exactly **why** we should do the things we must do, but we would know **that** we should do them. Unfortunately, however, the Moral Index version of Divine Command Theory is of little help since we are seldom able to determine "the commands of God."

In order to use God's commands as a measure of morality, we need to be able to do two different things. First, we must be able to determine the **identity** of those commands. But how are we to do this? Where are we to discover the commands of God? In the Bible? In the Koran? How about the various sacred Hindu texts, or the disputed gospels of St. Peter? Perhaps God's word is found in the pronouncements of "divinely inspired" prophets and religious leaders? But which prophets? Which religious leaders? Moses? Mohammed? The Pope? Martin Luther? The Dalai Lama? The local priest or rabbi? We could go on, but enough has been said to cast serious doubt on the claim that we can easily identify the commands of God. If these directives do exist, they are not so easily found as, say, the provisions of the Canadian Criminal Code or the American Bill of Rights. And a guide or index whose very identity is open to widespread dispute and controversy is of little use.

A second thing we must be able to do, if God's commands are to guide us morally, is to discern the **meaning** of those commands. Once we have identified a command as valid, we must be able to understand exactly what it says and how it applies to the innumerable situations in which we are faced with moral choices. But it is not at all obvious that we always have such understanding. Suppose we could all agree that some text or other contained the command of God on some moral matter. Take, for example, the Biblical commandment requiring that we honour our fathers and mothers. What exactly does it mean to honour our parents? Does this mean **always** obeying their wishes? If my mother wishes me to be a doctor, must I pursue this profession even though I'd rather be a professional hockey player and have the talent to succeed? If my mother disapproves of my choice of marriage partner, must I respect her wishes and run the risk of a miserable life? If not, then what exactly must I do, in such contexts, to honour my mother? What if my father wishes me to do something I consider **immoral**, like assault the neighbour's cat? Do I dishonour my father if I refuse to break Sylvester's leg? On what basis do I establish that assaulting the neighbour's cat **is** immoral? Must I find another of God's commands? But which one? And how do I determine which of the two competing commands takes precedence in this case? How do I determine whether to obey the command to honour my father, or to obey the command to avoid harming innocent animals? Consider now a more serious example: the Biblical injunction "Thou shalt not kill." Does this injunction apply to killing in self defence? If not, why not? Does it cover state sponsored execution? Most countries think that it does cover this activity and refuse to engage in it. Many American states think otherwise. How do we tell which parties are right? How do we come up with the correct **interpretation** of this particular command? At the end of the day, I cannot determine whether the Biblical injunction against killing extends to execution without entertaining questions about the value of human life and the competing interests at stake whenever it is under threat. I cannot, in other words, entertain such questions without engaging in moral reflection—i.e., some form of **moral reasoning** which is grounded in something other than the commands of God whose meaning is in question. So even if we believe that God's word is a guide to the requirements of morality, it seems clear that it cannot be a **sufficient** guide. We must, if we are to solve disputes about the identity and meaning of God's commands, engage in a form of moral reasoning which is independent of God's will. In short, the Moral Index version of Divine Command theory presupposes an independent theory of morality and moral reasoning upon the basis of which we can identify and interpret God's commands.

So the Divine Command theory, in all its forms, seems to suffer from serious difficulty. This has led some theologically inclined scholars to opt for a completely different theory of morality. One such theory is Natural Law theory of the sort identified with St. Thomas Aquinas. Although Aquinas does find an important place within his theory for God's commands, it is a limited place. For the most part, Aquinas' views on the nature of morality are much more in line with Leibniz's view that there are "rules of goodness and perfection in the nature of things."

Natural Law Theories

As with many philosophical labels, it is very difficult to provide a precise definition of "natural law theory." Its adherents are numerous and range from classical writers such as Plato, Aristotle, Cicero, and of course Aquinas, to contemporary writers as different as John Finnis, Lon Fuller and, arguably, Ronald Dworkin.[6] A further complication in coming to an understanding of natural law theory is that its adherents draw no radical distinction between law and morality. Law is, for these writers, an institutionalized form of morality—the result of an attempt to embody the moral law in concrete human practices. One important result of all this is that it is impossible to gain an understanding of the natural law theory of **morality** without at the same time exploring the natural law theory of legal systems. And we will not here attempt the impossible. Though our focus will remain on morality, we will of necessity be considering a good deal of what Aquinas has to say about human legal systems.

The Natural Law Theory of St. Thomas Aquinas

According to Aquinas, there is a law governing the universe which is universal, unchanging, rational and objective. This **Eternal Law** is God's rational plan or direction for all things within the universe. It includes the physical laws which govern the behaviour of inanimate objects, the laws which govern animal behaviour, as well as the moral, natural law which governs the conduct of rational creatures. It is "the plan of government in the Chief Governor," the rational plan God has for the orderly unfolding of the entire universe.[7] It always exists—that's why it is called Eternal Law—and its application is universal. It governs all things and events within the universe. Following Aristotle, Aquinas believed that all things have ends towards which they are naturally inclined, and it is the Eternal Law which directs a particular thing towards its natural ends. Morality, in this view, is a subset of the Eternal Law which applies to rational creatures like us. We, as rational human beings, have our own distinctive natural inclinations, as well as those we share with other things within the universe. Morality is therefore grounded in the very nature of the universe and in the authority of God, who is responsible for its creation and regulation. It is not, as the Subjectivist claims, a function of personal human choice, and it is not, as the Moral Conventionalist asserts, a function of societal or cultural choices. Nor is it, as the Moral Grounds version of the Divine Command theory implies, entirely dependent on God's naked will.

Aquinas says that it is of the essence of law, and hence the natural law, that it be promulgated or communicated. In saying this, he does not mean to suggest that every law must be promulgated to everything within the universe. A law needs to be communicated only to those entities which it governs. That part of the Eternal Law which deals with the behaviour of animals, for example, is promulgated to them through natural instinct. When animals follow their instincts, which they have no choice but to do, they are following that part of the Eternal Law which concerns them. They are not aware that they are doing so, but they do so nonetheless. The same is true for other biological entities like plants and trees. When a tree sheds its leaves in autumn it follows that part of the Eternal Law which governs its activities. Inanimate objects likewise follow the Eternal Law by observing physical laws — e.g., the laws of planetary motion or the laws governing the behaviour of elementary particles. The laws of physics, biology, animal behaviour and so on are, on Aquinas' conception, as much a part of the Eternal Law as is the Moral Natural Law.

With human beings, however, the situation is very different. Promulgation is a much richer activity. It is far superior in two important respects. First, we have (or can have) conscious awareness of the Eternal Law as it applies to our behaviour. Second, we also have the capacity to **choose** whether or not to observe the Eternal Law. Unlike a planet which is unaware that it is observing the laws of planetary motion and which cannot help but do so, we can know the Eternal Law which applies to us and choose whether or not to observe it. We have, in short, rationality and free will. This is what makes us moral beings.

That part of the Eternal Law which applies to our behaviour is promulgated to us in two different ways: the Natural Law and the Divine Law. The Natural Law is, Aquinas believes, "imprinted on us" (35). It is that part of the Eternal Law which governs the activities of rational human beings, and it can be known or apprehended by way of reason, by what Descartes many centuries later called "the light of nature." Through the exercise of their reason human beings can discover the natural laws governing their behaviour, and in so doing they can discover how morally they ought to live and behave. And because they have free will, they can choose whether or not to live and behave that way. The most basic principles of the Natural Law are, in Aquinas's view, self-evident. They are on a par with other truths of reason like the law of non-contradiction,[8] or the law which proclaims "Nihil ex Nihilo," that nothing can come from nothing. These principles of the Natural Law guide human beings towards their natural ends, ends towards which they are naturally inclined.

Although the basis for his distinction is not abundantly clear, Aquinas draws an important distinction between two different types or categories of Natural Laws: the **primary** and the **secondary** principles of the Natural Law. Among the primary principles is one basic principle from which all the other primary and secondary principles are thought by Aquinas to follow. Let's call this **The Fundamental Principle of the Natural Law**.

> **FP:** That good is to be done and pursued, and evil is to be avoided. (47)

Although it is the most basic of Aquinas' principles, FP tells us precious little about what we ought to do. In fact, it may well be an empty tautology, since it is plausible to think that part of the very meaning of the word "good" is that the entity so designated is to be done or pursued, and that part of the very meaning of the word "evil" is that the entity so deemed is to be avoided. But this poses little difficulty for Aquinas, since he goes on to provide substantive content to his fundamental principle by invoking Aristotle's teleological metaphysics.[9] Following Aristotle Aquinas holds, not only that all types of things within the universe are naturally inclined towards certain states, but that the good for an entity of some particular type is to be defined or understood in terms of those natural inclinations and the end states towards which they are inclined. Simplifying somewhat, we can say that:

> X is good for S if either: (1) X is an end towards which S is naturally inclined; or (2) X is a means of achieving Y and Y is an end towards which S is naturally inclined.

Some inclinations are more basic than others, and therefore some natural laws—i.e., those which concern themselves with those inclinations—are more basic than others. According to Aquinas, some of our very basic inclinations are ones which we, as human beings, share with all other things in the universe; these serve as the foundation for certain primary principles of the Natural Law. According to Aquinas, humankind

> seeks the preservation of its own being according to its nature, and by reason of this inclination, whatever is a means of preserving human life and of warding off its obstacles belongs to the natural law. (48)

There are also inclinations which human beings share with animals but not with other species, like trees and planets. He mentions sexual intercourse, the education of offspring, the pursuit of knowledge, and the inclination to live in society (48). Given these inclinations, certain basic principles of the natural law can be derived from FP. For example, it is a primary principle of the Natural Law that:

NL1: We ought to preserve our own well being. (47-48)

It is also a natural law that:

NL2: We ought to live in society. (47-48)

These primary principles of the Natural Law follow from FP, an Aristotelean teleological conception of the universe, and premises describing one or more of our very basic inclinations, many of which we share with other species of things.

In addition to FP and the Primary Principles of the Natural Law, there are "Secondary Principles of the Natural Law." Where exactly we are to draw the line between the primary and secondary principles is neither clear nor of much importance to us. But what is both clear and important is that the secondary principles:

a. are more detailed and concrete than primary principles

b. are more difficult to grasp

c. are logically entailed by the primary ones, and

d. can, like the primary principles, ultimately be traced back to FP and our natural inclinations.

Even more important, perhaps, is the following point.

e. Whereas the primary principles are self evident to all rational creatures, the secondary principles are "not equally known to all." (51)

Unlike the primary principles which "can nowise be blotted out from men's hearts" (55) the secondary principles can in a sense be prevented from emerging to consciousness by what Aquinas calls "evil persuasions," "vicious customs" and "corrupt habits" (55). They can also be prevented from emerging by less odious mistakes of reasoning, such as mistakes in logic. So some people, including whole cultures and societies, might lack awareness of some secondary principles of the Natural Law. They might, therefore, morally endorse corrupt practices which, in actual fact, violate the Natural Law. Among the so called "vicious customs" and "corrupt habits" historically condemned by some proponents of Natural Law Theory were things like homosexuality, abortion, and sexual activity outside marriage. In the view of some advocates, such practices are based on "unnatural" inclinations and therefore run afoul of Natural Law.[10] The fact that secondary principles of the Natural Law can be "blotted from men's hearts" by such "unnatural" inclinations will figure prominently in any attempt to explain the existence of "corrupt" practices. It will also figure in any attempt to explain the features of moral life seized upon by the Moral Relativist in defence of her view—e.g., that there appears to be widespread differences of opinion on moral matters. Much of this will be explained by pointing out the tendency of unnatural inclinations (and the corrupt practices to which they lead) to suppress the secondary principles of the Natural Law. But this tendency does not extend to the primary principles of the Natural Law according to Aquinas. Everyone, everywhere and at all times, knows them to be true, even if they choose to flout or ignore them by behaving badly.

Divine Law

Despite the existence of Natural Law, Aquinas thought, we also have need of a very different kind of law. Unlike Natural Law, which is promulgated to us through our capacity to reason, Divine Law is a set of standards explicitly revealed by God. It is revealed in much the same way as all moral standards are revealed to us on the Divine Command Theory, through authoritative pronouncements and texts. So its promulgation is more direct. We don't discover Divine Law by reasoning about matters. Rather, we are directly informed as to what we ought to do, much as we are when Parliament or Congress enacts a statute. Examples of Divine Law include, as one might expect, the Ten Commandments, and any scriptures or prophecies which religious authorities view as the revealed word of God. Aquinas cites two main reasons why Divine Law is necessary.

First, the Natural Law directs us towards our **natural** ends which, following Aristotle, Aquinas collects under the category of human happiness.[11] Our human reason is capable of grasping these natural ends and the Natural Law which follows from them. But it was also part of Aquinas' conception of the universe that human beings have a **supernatural** end which human reason is incapable of grasping in anything but the most rudimentary of ways. As a consequence, God must, Aquinas thought, command us more directly by simply telling us how to conduct ourselves. This he does via the Divine Law.

A second reason why Divine Law is necessary is that it is an essential **corrective** for our tendency to make errors in deriving secondary principles of the NL from primary ones.

> In order, therefore, that man may know without any
> doubt what he ought to do and what he ought to avoid,
> it was necessary for man to be directed in his proper
> acts by a law given by God, for it is certain that such a
> law cannot err. (23)

So the DL acts as a **supplement** to the Natural Law insofar
as it concerns supernatural ends beyond the scope of the
Natural Law. It also serves as a **corrective** insofar as it serves
to correct our mistakes in deriving, via fallible human reason
and subject to the influence of evil habits and persuasions,
the Natural Law as it applies to our conduct. Were people
perfectly rational and capable of rising above the corrupt-
ing influence of evil customs and habits, the Divine Law
would not be necessary as a corrective and we could derive,
for any situation with which we were faced, the Natural Law
applying to that situation. We could, in other words, through
the exercise of reason, always determine our moral rights,
duties and obligations. But we're not perfectly rational, so
God must sometimes tell us directly what to do. Of course,
determining what that is can, as we saw earlier, be a difficult
matter. God's commands are subject to the problems of
identity and the problems of interpretation and application
outlined above.

Human Law

For a variety of reasons canvassed by Aquinas, not even
Natural and Divine Law working in unison are sufficient to
guide human conduct fully. Human law is also essential for
human flourishing, including our flourishing as moral beings.
At one point Aquinas notes, once again following Aristotle,
that human beings have a natural aptitude for virtue, but that

the perfection of virtue must be acquired by means of some kind of training.[12] Some people do not receive the requisite training, however, and are therefore "prone to vice" (57). These, Aquinas believes, must be restrained from moral evil by the force of human law. It is in the very nature of human law to help bring about compliance with God's moral law.

So human law is an institution whose primary aim is to help people become virtuous — to become moral. Laws enacted by a human sovereign, and backed by sufficient force to ensure compliance, are essential if some people — those whose inclination to virtue has not been developed by proper training — are to acquire the appropriate habits of living in accordance with Natural and Divine Law, while those whose training leads them voluntarily to do so are to be left in peace. This picture of human law highlights a crucial feature of Aquinas' conception of human law. Human law is not something entirely divorced from morality. On the contrary, it is a means by which human beings may be made to comply with the Natural and Divine Law, and its authority as law derives from the authority of God.

So it is part of Eternal Law that there should be a human sovereign who enacts human laws in accordance with Natural Law. But what sorts of laws is the sovereign to enact? How does he know which laws to create? The answer is simple: he exercises reason and determines what is for the common good in the circumstances in which his society finds itself. He derives human laws from the Natural Law. According to Aquinas this derivation can take two forms — logical deduction and what Aquinas calls the "determination of common notions." He writes:

> ... it must be noted that something may be derived
> from the natural law in two ways: first, as a conclusion

from premises; secondly, by way of determination of certain generalities.[13] (59)

Here's an example of deduction:

1. One should harm no person. (A primary principle of the Natural Law)

2. To kill a person is to harm him. (A natural fact about the world)

3. Therefore, one should kill no person. (A secondary principle of the Natural Law)

Statement 3 serves as the basis for various human laws against killing.

Determination is quite different from pure deduction in that it leaves considerably more room for creativity on the part of the sovereign. Although Aquinas thinks that the primary (and perhaps even the secondary) principles of the natural law hold for everyone at all times—i.e. they are universal in their application—"particular determinations" of these principles often vary according to time and circumstance. This is one reason why human laws, as well as many of the moral practices cited by defenders of Moral Relativism, vary from time to time and place to place—and an additional reason why Human Law is necessary. It is necessary to determine, i.e., render more determinate, what the Natural Law leaves open.

An example which illustrates determination of generalities or common notions can be found in a typical **co-ordination problem,** like the problem of settling on which side of the road everyone is to drive on. Presumably the Natural

Law is indeterminate with respect to whether we should drive on the right or drive on the left, but it is essential that we all co-ordinate our activities in some way. If some of us are going to drive on one particular side of the road, then it is crucial that we all do so. Since there are many different solutions to this co-ordination problem, each of which is consistent with the Natural Law, a choice must somehow be made among them. Human reason does not tell us **which** choice to make, though it does tell us that a choice has to be made.[14] And for this we need a sovereign who has "care of the community." The sovereign must make the choice for us, must render one of the available options **salient,** i.e., that option which the Natural Law requires us to respect once the sovereign has chosen it for us.

In explaining the nature of determination Aquinas draws on the analogy of a builder (59) who is constrained in building a house to observe certain guidelines—e.g., there must be walls and a roof, and perhaps rooms. But the size of the walls, the kind of roof and how many rooms can be matters of determination. This is not to say that the builder has unfettered discretion in these matters. He will have to work within the budget assigned, bear in mind the needs of the prospective occupants, and he cannot, e.g., create a house with 250 rooms if he has only 700 square metres of floor space with which to work. But within a range of reasonable alternatives, set by the common form of a house and the particular circumstances under which he pursues his craft, it is up to the builder to determine the exact features of the house he will build. The same is true of the sovereign in his pursuit of laws which conform with the Natural Law. The primary and secondary principles of the Natural Law are objectively binding for every sovereign in every circumstance, but certain more specific matters of determination are subject to his creative choice.

So the Natural Law is indifferent between driving on the right and driving on the left. But as soon as one of these two options is "laid down" by a sovereign, action in accordance with that option becomes a matter of justice which the Natural Law requires that we observe. Similar things can be said about conventional moral practices lying outside the scope of Human Law. The sovereign may not—perhaps should not—concern himself with whether women should, as a sign of respect, remove their hats before entering a place of worship such as a church, synagogue or mosque. The Natural (and perhaps Divine) Law may require that respect be shown, but it may well leave it to local **custom** or **convention** to determine exactly how that respect is to be shown. One society or culture may make the "determination" that respect requires the doffing of hats, while another culture might require the exact opposite. In each case, local custom or convention serves the role played by Aquinas' sovereign in "determining" the "common notions" of the Moral Law. And in each case we have a powerful explanation of moral diversity which is consistent with an objectively valid, universal law. We have, in short, a plausible answer to the Diversity Argument in favour of Moral Relativism.

If this extension of Aquinas' theory to conventional practices accurately reflects the theoretical structure of Natural Law Theory, then its proponents are not necessarily forced to deny the insights upon which the Relativist's Diversity Argument relies. The Discretion Theory of determination allows the Natural Lawyer to maintain his belief in universally valid moral standards in the face of significant diversity in moral practices. This seldom acknowledged feature of Natural Law theory is a highly attractive one which could, and probably should, be incorporated into any moral theory. Any theorist would do well to consider seriously the possibility that morality is a blend of objectively valid, universal standards, and particular determinations of these "common notions."

Concluding Remarks

Aquinas' theory of determination, together with his views on how derivations from the Natural Law can go wrong, provide us with a powerful means of addressing the Diversity Argument upon which the case for Moral Relativism largely rests. Aquinas is happy to acknowledge that human laws and conventional moral practices are often in violation of natural law. He is also happy to acknowledge that large parts of human law and morality concern matters about which the Natural Law is indifferent. So there is nothing in Natural Law Theory which excludes the possibility that different environments, including different social environments, might yield, in combination with the same fundamental Natural Laws, very different legal and moral standards. One might question whether Aquinas has gone far enough in recognizing the extent to which moral and legal practices differ, but there is no doubt that he does go quite a way along this line.

Despite this, the suspicion may linger that proponents of the Diversity Argument are on to a very important point which cuts to the very heart of debates concerning the status of morality. We might all agree with Aquinas' fundamental principle of the Natural Law (that good ought to be pursued, and evil avoided) if only because it is little more than an empty tautology. But perhaps this is as far as we could get in reaching agreement. Perhaps people's "inclinations" vary so dramatically (think of the vastly different inclinations

of Pope John Paul II and Madonna) that it is implausible to
suppose that we are all somehow united in our essential natures and, therefore, our "natural inclinations." Indeed, there
may be nothing we could reasonably call "human nature"
from which we could derive much of anything at all. Perhaps,
as many feminists assert, what is taken to be "natural" is in
large measure a function of a male-centred, patriarchal perspective which has dominated human culture for millennia.[15]
According to many social and political theorists, there is no
such thing as a common human nature, only a wide range
of vastly different "socially constructed" natures or identities
upon the basis of which much oppression has thrived. Yet
if we do not share a common nature and common inclinations, then how can there be a universal moral law based on
these things? Views on what is natural, good and right do, of
course, vary considerably, and so one might agree that it is at
the very least problematic to suppose that there are universal
principles of conduct binding on all rational creatures at all
times and in all places. But once again there is reason to be
cautious in deriving any such skeptical conclusions in favour
of Moral Relativism. There may yet be a commonality lurk-
ing behind our undoubted differences. If we could discover
what that is, perhaps we could, in conjunction with a theory
of determination and a theory of moral mistakes, come up
with a plausible theory of morality.

    Aquinas' theory is based on the authority of God and
a robust metaphysical view about the nature of the entire
universe: that all things within the universe of God's creation have natural ends, as well as natural inclinations towards
those ends which can serve to guide us in discovering God's
Eternal Law. In particular, these can guide us in discovering
the Natural Law which applies to rational creatures like us.
From this Natural Law we can derive (by way of deduction

and determination) both the content of our legal systems and the requirements of morality. If we reject this blend of Christian theology and Aristotelean metaphysics, then we have of course rejected the very foundation of Aquinas' theory. But the question arises: Could we substitute a different theology and a different metaphysical view? Could a non-theist, who rejected all talk of natural inclinations and an essential human nature still pursue a natural law account of morality? Perhaps, but if the theory is to be a recognizably natural law account, it will have to share with Aquinas' theory at least two key features. First, it will have to support the premise that there are at least **some** universal, objective truths about what is good for human beings from which it is possible to derive standards governing human conduct. Second, it will have to be coupled with an epistemology according to which these truths are in some way discoverable by human reason. In other words, the Natural Law theory we end up with must reject any robust form of Moral Relativism on which moral judgments express nothing more than individual preferences or emotions or simply assert what is in accordance with cultural conventions. It will also have to reject the claim that moral reasoning is incapable of adjudicating among competing standards of morality. There is still going to have to be a basis for the claim that at least some moral standards are in some sense objectively and universally valid, and that we can discover what these are by engaging in moral reasoning. One important attempt to provide such a basis lies in social contract theory. Social contract theories do not deny that we differ dramatically in our interests and inclinations. But they would have us believe that there are certain things which we nevertheless do share in common—the desire to survive and to flourish in close proximity with each other. From this particular basis, social contract theories attempt to derive morality from prudence. Morality is, on this particular conception, the result of a kind of agreement or contract with which rational agents out to secure their own interests would agree. It is to this theory that we now turn.

Notes

1. Numerous editions and translations of all three works are available in print. Plato wrote in the fifth century, B.C. and Aquinas in the thirteenth century, A.D. Leibniz's *Discourse on Metaphysics* was published in 1686. For purposes of discussion, we will assume in this chapter that God exists. If there is no God, then Divine Command theory must, of course, be rejected. Whether Natural Law theory can survive without the existence of God is a difficult question to answer.

2. For reasons to be considered shortly, this particular theory may, in truth, not be a version of Divine Command Theory at all.

3. The Principles of Perfection are not confined to moral standards, but include, for example, what we would be more inclined to call aesthetic standards. We can, however, safely ignore this complication.

4. Leibniz, *Discourse on Metaphysics*, as found in Steven Cahn (Ed.), *Classics of Western Philosophy*, 5th ed. (Indianapolis: Hackett Publishing, 1999), p. 463.

5. For further argument see Plato's *Euthyphro*.

6. See John Finnis, *Natural Law and Natural Rights* (Oxford: Oxford University Press, 1980); Lon Fuller, *The Morality of Law* (New Haven: Yale University Press, 1964); Ronald Dworkin, *Law's Empire* (Cambridge: Harvard University Press, 1986).

7. This and all other direct references to Aquinas' *Summa* are taken from a collection edited by W.P. Baumgarth and R.J. Regan entitled *Saint Thomas Aquinas: On Law, Morality and Politics* (Indianapolis: Hackett, 1988). This particular quotation is from p. 37. All future references to Aquinas that are included within the text are, unless otherwise indicated, taken from the Baumgarth and Regan collection.

8. The law of non-contradiction is often held to be one of the fundamental principles governing all forms of human reason. According to this law, nothing can be both F and non-F, e.g., be square and not-square, at one and the same time.

9. For further discussion of Aristotle's teleological conception of the universe, see Chapter 9 below.

10. According to many critics, the fact that such practices are so easily targeted as "unnatural" reveals an inherent danger in Natural Law Theory. Any activity which a person or society wishes to suppress, particularly activities engaged in by minority groups, can be easily condemned as "unnatural" and therefore immoral. Furthermore, as many feminists argue, the "natural" has too often been equated with whatever serves the interests of males, and the "unnatural" is too easily equated with the "unusual" or the "different."

11. On this see Chapter 9 below.

12. Again, this aspect of Aristotle's theory will be discussed more fully in Chapter 9 below.

13. In other translations the term "common notions" is substituted for the term "generalities." We will treat these terms as equivalent in meaning.

14. It is possible that reason could, in certain special circumstances, suggest one alternative over another. If, over a significant period of time, a social convention has begun to emerge that leads people to drive on the left, then it might be unreasonable for the sovereign to legislate against this emerging social convention by requiring that we drive on the right. But often times there is no established or emerging convention one way or the other, and hence no reason to prefer one option over another.

15. See Chapter 10 below.

Five
The Social Contract Theory of Morality[1]

Traditional Social Contract Theory

Social Contract Theory came to prominence in the seventeenth and eighteenth centuries as a political philosophy. Its aim was to explain and justify the state, as well as the basis and extent of our political (and legal) obligations. This theory, associated with influential philosophers like Thomas Hobbes, John Locke, and Jean Jacques Rousseau, views law and society as products of an actual (or hypothetical) "social contract" among rational, self-interested individuals.[2] Sovereign kings, queens and legislative bodies do not possess their authority to govern by Divine Right—by the command of God. Nor is any particular person or body naturally entitled or suited to rule by natural law. Rather whatever authority the sovereign possesses is the result of a social contract to which he is an important party. This social contract **grants** authority to the sovereign—it "empowers" or authorizes the sovereign to govern on behalf of a community.[3] But why would rationally, self-interested individuals enter into any such contract with a sovereign? Why would they grant this person or body the normative power to impose, and enforce physically if necessary, duties on them? The answer lies in the following considerations.

Though there is much more that separates individuals from each other than Aquinas seems to acknowledge, these differences are greatly overshadowed by a few key facts about human beings and the world they inhabit. First, there is a **basic equality** among people, both in terms of their basic needs and desires and in terms of their abilities to fulfil those needs and desires. For example, although some of us are stronger or smarter than others, no one's superiority in these respects is sufficient to overcome a group of other people should they band together to assert themselves. Tom might be the strongest of the group, but he will never be strong enough to ward off the attacks of his five neighbours working in concert. Eventually they will be able to thwart his efforts to assert himself over them. Among the basic desires which unify us is the basic **desire to survive in close proximity with one another**. This, of course, is a desire (or inclination) upon which Aquinas constructed a good deal of his Natural Law theory. Virtually all contract theorists would reject Aquinas' full blown teleological conception of human nature and its place within the universe. But they would all agree with Aquinas that each of us wants to survive and is intelligent and far-sighted enough to see that this interest is furthered by the existence of government and the force of law. These are essential if we are to have a reasonable chance of surviving and fulfilling our basic needs as well as whatever desires and ambitions we happen to have.

A second basic fact of the world we inhabit is a **scarcity of goods**. The material things we need to survive and flourish are not in such plentiful supply that we needn't worry about getting what we need (or desire). The essentials of life do not just grow on the trees, waiting for us to pick them. But equally important is the fact that the degree of scarcity is not so severe that there is no hope of ever getting what we need. Were it the case that, no matter what we did together, there would still not be nearly enough to go around, we might not be inclined to cooperate with one another to ensure that each of us gets what he needs. But there is (or so the social contract theorists thought) enough to go around if people cooperate with one another. The fostering of this cooperation is one of the reasons people band together under the terms of a social contract.

Next, there is the fact that we are neither devils nor saints — that we possess **limited altruism**. Were we all saints, then perhaps we could always rely on each other to see that our basic needs and desires are met. Each of us would be our neighbour's keeper. Were we all devils, out to thwart the interests of others whenever we got the chance, then perhaps no cooperative enterprise like the social contract could work. Whatever its nature, and whatever the physical means by which it is enforced, a social contract requires some modest level of voluntary cooperation and self sacrifice. In order to reap the long term benefits of the social contract, we must sometimes sacrifice our immediate wants and desires, and we must be able to trust that others will do their bit in return. Were we all devils, such trust would not be possible. So the fact that we possess, or are at least capable of displaying, limited altruism is an essential ingredient of traditional social contract theory.

Finally, there is the fact that we display **practical rationality** and are therefore able to reason about practical matters such as how we might improve our lot in life. We can contemplate not only how things are, but how they might be improved upon. David Gauthier, the contemporary philosopher whose modern social contract theory we will explore below, expresses this aspect of human nature by claiming that we are capable of "semantic representation."[4] As semantic representers, we are able to represent states of affairs to ourselves, and critically reflect upon these states of affairs. By critically reflecting on these represented states of affairs, we are able to consider whether they are or are not the case, and further, whether or not we would **want** them to be the case. In this way, we are capable of representing not only factual states of affairs (Paris is in France) but desired states of affairs as well (I would rather be in Paris, France). This leads to a second component of Gauthier's views on our practical rationality: in virtue of our ability to represent our desires (or preferences) semantically and to reflect upon them critically, our desires can become ordered "in relation to decision and action, so that we may choose to **maximize** our expectation of desire-fulfilment."[5] In other words, we are able to reason about the probabilities and "utilities" associated with the various outcomes of the various actions, plans of action, and strategies we might undertake, and act in a way that we believe will give us the best chance of seeing our desires and needs fulfilled.[6] These features of our practical rationality allow us to reason ourselves out of situations in which our expected utilities are less than they might be. In particular, we are able to use reason and foresight to determine how best to extricate ourselves from what traditional social contract theorists called "the state of nature."

The State of Nature

Imagine a world with no government, no law courts, no police, and no means of ensuring that whatever co-operative arrangements we might make with each other are respected.

What would life be like in such a world? According to Thomas Hobbes, life would be pretty awful. In his classic work *Leviathan* Hobbes describes this world, which he calls "the state of nature." There is, in the state of nature,

> no place for industry, because the fruit thereof is un-
> certain, and consequently no culture of the earth; no
> navigation, nor use of the commodities that may be
> imported by sea; no commodious building; no instru-
> ments of moving and removing such things as require
> much force; no knowledge of the face of the earth; no
> account of time; no arts; no letters; no society; and,
> which is worst of all, continual fear and danger of
> violent death; and the life of man solitary, poor, nasty,
> brutish, and short.[7]

Given the facts of relative scarcity and equality, and (very) limited altruism, the state of nature is, for Hobbes, a world of continual war of each against the others. It is a dangerous and ruthlessly competitive world in which there is no peace and in which all those material, intellectual and spiritual things upon which we have come to rely and which require, for their existence, some measure of trust and co-operation would simply not be possible. Seeing the futility of life in the state of nature, rational, self-interested individuals will be led to the inevitable conclusion that they are better off living in a soci-ety with law and a political structure. Their expected utilities are far greater in such a world than could ever be the case in the state of nature. They will see the wisdom of surrendering their (largely worthless) liberties to a sovereign, empowered to set the terms upon which peace and co-operation can be allowed to flourish. It was Hobbes' view that escaping the state of nature requires that each social contractor surrender every one of his "natural rights" to liberty (which, in the state of nature, essentially entitle him to do whatever will promote his particular interests, even if this means harming or killing others). The one exception is the right to self defence which no rational being could ever surrender. Since the most fundamental aim of the social contract is the achievement of survival in close proximity with one another, it would not be rational, Hobbes thought, to surrender that right by entering the social contract. But if we are all to survive, we must, Hobbes thought, give up all of our other liberties. We must authorize or empower a sovereign to rule over us in whatever way he sees fit. Unless he threatens our survival, life under the sovereign's rule, regardless of what he requires of us, is better than the state of nature. Hence we need political and legal systems in which voluntary compliance by law-abiding citizens is backed up and supplemented by the coercive force of the law.

Modern Social Contract Theories of Morality

Although its origins lie in political philosophy, attempts have been made in recent years to adapt traditional social contract theory to explain and justify morality. Morality, on these modified social contract theories, is a set of standards which would be agreed upon by rationally self-interested individuals smart enough to realize the benefits of living in a society in which these standards are observed.[8] Viewed in this way, the standards of morality can be derived from prudence or self interest.[9] This feature of the Social Contract theory of morality results in a number of advantages. First, we have a ready answer to the question: Why should I be moral? One should be moral, according to the Social Contract theorist, because it is ultimately in one's rational self-interest to be so. Superficial appearances to the contrary, morality actually works to my own personal advantage. It is not something which fundamentally works against my natural inclination to seek the fulfilment of my own selfish desires and interests.[10] Second, in accounting for the validity of moral standards, we do not have to posit anything more mysterious or contentious than a small number of basic desires (e.g., the desire to survive and the desire to fulfil one's basic physiological needs for things like food and shelter) together with a basic theory of instrumental rationality which can be used to determine which moral standards would be to the advantage of each rationally self-interested social contractor. We do not, in other words, have to posit anything like Aquinas' principles of the natural law which human reason is supposed to be able to discover and grasp in the same way that it is able to discover and grasp the basic principles of logic. A third advantage of the theory is that it is able to accommodate the insights of the moral relativist while at the same time asserting that there must be at least a common core of morality which is universal across various times and cultures. To the extent that the prudential needs and interests of individuals are uniform across different times and cultures, the standards of morality based on these interests will be universal too. Those standards may well be subject to Aquinas' "determination of common notions," but the standards to be so interpreted will be universal. On the other hand, to the extent that many of our wants, desires and interests vary from time to time, culture to culture, and person to person, the standards of morality can vary accordingly. Social Contract theory is quite capable, therefore, of finding a suitable mid-point between a robust moral relativism, on the one hand, and a full blown moral objectivism of the sort represented by Aquinas' natural law theory, on the other.

David Gauthier develops an ethical theory on which morality can fruitfully be understood as a manifestation of rational choice. Morality is not something which competes with rational self-interest, requiring that we routinely sacrifice our own interests for those of others. On the contrary, it is what rational people would ultimately agree upon were they faced with the prospects of living in the state of nature. In developing his moral theory, Gauthier employs a heuristic device known as the **Prisoner's Dilemma**. Morality is, in his view, a rational means of escaping real world versions of the Prisoner's Dilemma. It is a way of escaping the state of nature in which, as Hobbes observed, life would be solitary, poor, nasty, brutish, and short.

The Prisoner's Dilemma

Consider the following scenario. You and Ted have each been apprehended and charged in connection with the same crime and are taken to separate rooms to be interviewed. In the course of your interrogation you learn the following facts. If you confess to the crime but Ted does not, you will get a one year prison sentence. Ted, on the other hand, will be put away for ten years. You also learn that if you do not confess while Ted does, it will be **you** who gets the ten year sentence and Ted who gets off with only one year. Furthermore, you learn that if **both** of you confess to the crime, each one of you will get five years in the slammer—**and** that if **neither** of you confesses, the authorities will have enough to put each of you away for only two years. Finally, although you are unable to communicate with Ted, you do know that he is rational and that he has managed to put together the same information as you have. In this scenario you and Ted are faced with what is known as the Prisoner's Dilemma.

Five :: *The Social Contract Theory of Morality*

The Prisoner's Dilemma

		Ted	
		Confess	Do not confess
You	Confess	5,5	1,10
	Do not confess	10,1	2,2

- 1st number in box: your time in jail.
- 2nd number in box: Ted's time in jail.

It is clear that the optimal scenario is for you and Ted both to clam up. However, since neither of you can be sure what the other will do (remember, you cannot communicate with one another) you will both be led to reason as follows. "If he confesses, then I had better confess too, otherwise I'm in for ten years. If, on the other hand, he does not confess, then I am still better off confessing: I'll be out in a year instead of two. So, whatever he does, I'm better off if I confess." Since this conclusion will be the one to which each of you is rationally drawn, each of you will end up confessing. And each of you will end up doing five years—this despite the fact that if you had both refused to confess, you would each have got away with only two years! This, of course, has the look of paradox: how can each person, making what, from his perspective, is the only rational choice, end up worse off than he might have been had he made a different, supposedly non-rational choice? How can each person, acting rationally, end up worse off? He's (apparently) better off acting irrationally! This feature displays what Gauthier calls the "structural problem of interaction" inherent in Prisoner's Dilemmas.[11] What appears to be the rational choice (confessing) results in a worse result (five years each) than the result associated with what appears to be the irrational choice (not confessing). This latter choice is one such that, if it could somehow be agreed upon by both parties, the result would be better or more optimal (two years apiece).

According to Gauthier, the structural problem inherent in the Prisoner's Dilemma reveals an important fact: the decision to confess only appears to be rational according to a strategy Gauthier calls **straightforward utility maximization**. You and Ted end up in the fix you do only because you are straightforward utility maximizers. A straightforward maximizer is one "who seeks to maximize his utility given the strategies of those with whom he interacts."[12] This is the rationale you and Ted use when each of you reasons: "Whatever he does, I am better off confessing." In order for the decision **not** to confess to be seen as the rational one to make, you need to be pursuing a different strategy. You need to choose on the basis of what Gauthier calls **constrained maximization**. A constrained maximizer is defined as "a person who seeks in some situations to maximize her utility, given not the strategies but the utilities of those with whom she interacts."[13] If you and Ted were focussing on the utilities associated with your decisions whether to confess or not, you would see that the rational thing to do is for both of you to refuse to confess. Of course, this would be rational for each of you only if one very important condition is observed: you must have reason to believe that the other party will come to the same decision. In other words, the rationality of constrained maximization holds only when one is interacting with others who are willing to cooperate. For this reason, the rationality of cooperating in a Prisoner's Dilemma situation depends, in the words of Gilbert Harman, "on the likelihood that one will be dealing with cooperators and the extent to which they can be recognized and distinguished from non-cooperators."[14] You and Ted had no idea what the other would do and were therefore forced to rely on straightforward utility maximization. It was therefore not rational for you to be constrained maximizers. And this led to the five-year terms. But in a scenario where you have good reason to believe that others will be constrained maximizers, you have reason to be a constrained maximizer as well.

Gauthier likens the situation in which you and Ted find yourselves to the natural, pre-social condition of humankind, sketched in such graphic detail by Hobbes. Morality, on Gauthier's account, acts as a **constraining** factor that enables us to overcome the structural problem of interaction illustrated by the Prisoner's Dilemma. Morality facilitates, or makes possible, the rational pursuit of constrained maximization, which leaves everyone better off. Just as you and Ted end up with two years instead of five if you cooperate, we end up, if we cooperate in adopting mutually binding moral constraints, with a world where life is not quite as solitary, poor, nasty, brutish, and short as Hobbes' state of nature. We in fact end up maximizing our individual expected utilities.

This, then, is the basis of morality on Gauthier's contemporary social contract theory. It is important to stress that Gauthier's primary concern is to "validate the conception of morality as a set of rational, impartial constraints on the pursuit of individual interest, not to defend any particular moral code."[15] In principle, then, Gauthier's theory is as compatible with Kantian deontology as it is with any number of consequentialist theories. This is not to say, however, that the theory provides no means of choosing among these competing normative theories. Indeed, the theory provides a potentially very useful means of influencing the desired choice: one can determine which standards of morality are justified by determining which constraints on the pursuit of straightforward utility maximization it would be reasonable to agree upon as a means of escaping Prisoner's Dilemma scenarios. Moral questions are reducible, in the end, to questions of practical rationality.

It is also important to stress that Gauthier's theory does not presuppose that there are any moral standards which exist independently of, or antecedent to, the social contract. The impartial constraints on the pursuit of individual self-interest characteristic of morality are **generated by** our rational response to the structures of interaction illustrated by the Prisoner's Dilemma. They are not imposed from the outset. Morality is not something which competes with practical rationality or prudence — it is a rational response to the natural, pre-social state in which we would find ourselves were we not to pursue the possibility of constrained maximization offered by morality.

Returning now to the Prisoner's Dilemma, we can see that the main obstacle preventing you and Ted from rationally choosing not to confess is the uncertainty surrounding the question whether the other party will also choose to stay silent. We can put it another way. Both you and Ted can see well enough that the optimal outcome in terms of total personal utility or self-interest results from the both of you not confessing. So you are both disposed **hypothetically** to agree to cooperate with one another in not confessing. You can both see that it would be rational for each of you to engage in a cooperative practice of constrained maximization that results in mutually advantageous outcomes. But this would be rational only if you can be reasonably certain that the other will cooperate. When is it rational to expect such compliance from other parties?

At this point, Gauthier parts company with Hobbes. According to Gauthier,

Hobbes' egoistic psychology allows internalization of no standard other than that of direct concern with individual preservation and contentment. And so it is only in so far as the sovereign is able to enforce the law that compliance with it is rationally binding on the individual.[16]

In other words, according to Hobbes it is rational to be a constrained maximizer, who cooperates with others in abandoning the unbridled pursuit of self-interest, only if there is a sovereign with sufficient power and might to **enforce** compliance, to make compliance the only rational avenue open to each of us. This, of course, is a political, not a moral solution. In Gauthier's view, our ability to look beyond straightforward maximization to the potential advantages of cooperative ventures enables us to transcend the limitations of Hobbes' egoistic psychology and to see that it can be rational to accept constrained maximization, even without the sovereign's threat.

> Constrained maximization thus links the idea of morals by agreement to actual moral practice. We suppose that some moral principles may be understood as representing joint strategies prescribed to each person as part of the ongoing cooperative arrangements that constitute society.[17]

So far we have seen how, in Gauthier's view, moral standards and the constraints dictated by the rationality of constrained maximization are in fact congruent. But there is still the question why it is rational to constrain one's unbridled pursuit of self-interest given the undeniable fact that there will always be others who will not cooperate, and who will therefore take advantage of one's restraint. Recall that it is rational not to confess only if you can be reasonably certain that Ted will do the same. But if that certainty is absent, the only rational thing to do is to confess, leading, of course, to the five-year jail sentence. Gauthier's solution to this crucial difficulty is essentially to treat constrained maximizers as belonging to a kind of club. He supposes that persons are sufficiently "translucent" to enable us to ascertain, more or less, their dispositions to cooperate.[18] This does not mean that constrained maximizers are always able to identify one another; they might on some occasions mistake a straightforward maximizer for one of their own. Conditions in the real world are not ideal. Nevertheless, there is a strategy that can be used to overcome this less than ideal situation. It is rational to dispose oneself to constrained maximization if straightforward maximizers are routinely excluded from the benefits of cooperation. If known straightforward maximizers are excluded from the benefits of club membership, the size of the club is likely to grow, and it will become safer and safer to be a constrained maximizer. Gauthier writes:

> [t]he essential point in our argument is that one's disposition to choose affects the situations in which one may expect to find oneself. A straightforward maximizer, who is disposed to make maximizing choices, must expect to be excluded from cooperative arrangements which he would find advantageous. A constrained maximizer may expect to be included in such arrangements. She benefits from her disposition, not in the choices she makes, but in her opportunities to choose.[19]

So straightforward maximizers can do better than they would through constrained maximization only if they capitalize on the disposition of constrained maximizers to cooperate. But if constrained maximizers exclude straightforward maximizers from their cooperative practices altogether, the former will be left to fend for themselves as individuals operating outside of any joint activities. But the utilities they can expect to achieve in such a scenario are not nearly as attractive as those enjoyed by constrained maximizers. Thus there is in truth no rational alternative but to dispose oneself to be a constrained maximizer. In this way, then, Gauthier manages to justify or warrant compliance with the strictures of constrained maximization, which have all the characteristics of what we think of as moral standards. Moral standards by their very nature typically call on us to constrain our pursuit of self-interest.

The Principle of Minimax Relative Concession

Having established that it is rational to cooperate for mutual advantage in observing moral constraints on straightforward utility maximization, we must recognize that there will always be a range of options open to us. Imagine that we are in a situation in which we are attempting to set the terms of our cooperative moral scheme. In bargaining among ourselves we will be led to consider a number of alternative "moral codes" and the question will inevitably arise: Which option(s) would it be rational for us to adopt? Everyone will, of course, occupy an initial bargaining position which, for our purposes, will consist of that person's utility level prior to any agreement reached. And everyone will be keen to make sure that he is not made worse off by any bargain which he might make. Given that the goal of the bargain is to make each of us better off, a successful agreement will necessarily result in what Gauthier calls a "cooperative surplus." That is, there will be more expected utility or value after the agreement is reached and acted upon, than there could possibly be were there no agreement at all.[20] But now the question arises: How is this cooperative surplus to be distributed among participants? There may be a range of agreements on which everyone is better off than before, but these might distribute the surplus in different ways. Under option 1, X may do slightly better than Y; under option 2, Y may do much better than X. On both options, X and Y are better off than they would have been without an agreement, but they will not benefit to the same extent. So how is a choice to be made? Consider the following example which serves to illustrate the problem and Gauthier's solution to it.

Howie and Sari want to go to a movie together. Each has an initial **claim** regarding the movie they should see together. Howie stakes a claim to seeing *Terminator*, while Sari's preference or claim is *The French Lieutenant's Woman*. Howie would derive 10 units of utility (enjoyment) from seeing *Terminator*, while Sari's utility would be 15.[21] On the other hand, Howie would derive only 3 units of utility from seeing *The French Lieutenant's Woman* while Sari, who just loves the movie, would garner a whopping 30 units of utility. If they fail to cooperate, going to no movie at all, each experiences no utility whatsoever. Their utility levels would then be 0. This represents their "initial bargaining positions." Now we are in a position to calculate the various **relative concessions** that Howie and Sari will have to accept, according to the choices and outcomes described above. Relative concession is the proportion that the **absolute magnitude** of the concession bears to the difference between the utility the person would derive from a particular decision and his utility in the initial bargaining position.[22] If they see *Terminator*, Howie's relative concession is 0 because it is his initial claim—he is not making any concession at all if they accept his claim and see *Terminator*. But Sari's is 50%—15/30—15 being the absolute magnitude of her concession (she gets 15 by seeing *Terminator* instead of the 30 she would get by seeing *The French Lieutenant's Woman*) and 30 being the difference between the utility she would enjoy were her initial claim fulfilled and the utility of the initial bargaining position. If they see *The French Lieutenant's Woman*, on the other hand, Howie's relative concession is 70%—7/10—7 being the absolute magnitude of his concession (he gets 3 by seeing *The French Lieutenant's Woman* instead of the 10 he would get by seeing *Terminator*). Sari's concession is, of course, 0 because seeing *The French Lieutenant's Woman* is **her** initial claim or preference. With this example in mind, we are now in a position to understand Gauthier's principle of **minimax relative concession**:

> the principle [states] that given a range of outcomes, each of which requires concessions by some or all persons if it is to be selected, then an outcome is to be selected only if the greatest **maximum** relative concession it requires is as small as possible, or a **minimum**, that is, no greater than the maximum relative concession required by each other outcome.[23]

According to the principle of minimax relative concession, the rational outcome of Howie's and Sari's situation is for them to see *Terminator*. The maximum relative concession would be only 50% (Sari's relative concession) instead of 70% (Howie's relative concession). In short, Sari concedes or gives up less by going to see *Terminator* than Howie would if they went to see *The French Lieutenant's Woman*.

It should now be easy to see how the principle of minimax relative concession bears on the rationality of complying with constrained maximization. Not every bargain in which overall utility is enhanced will be equally attractive to all parties. "Since no one chooses to constrain his behaviour for its own sake, no person finds it rational to be more compliant than his fellows."[24] So no rational bargainer will be willing to comply with just **any** cooperative arrangement which creates a cooperative surplus. It will be rational to compare cooperative schemes which create a surplus and to determine which schemes minimize the maximum concession required by each participant. Any cooperative scheme might be better than the state of nature. But it fails to follow that all schemes are equally worthy of support, and that there is no reason to prefer some over others.

Moral Progress

Gauthier's social contract theory provides us with a way of understanding morality as a rational response to Hobbes' state of nature. Rational creatures capable of semantic representation and reflective, practical rationality will see the wisdom of observing moral constraints on straightforward utility maximization. As rational creatures, then, we are able to view or conceive the moral standards by which we actually live in society as being capable of rational defence. But just as we are able to conceive of our existing world with its existing moral standards as an alternative to the state of nature, we can also compare our existing world with alternative worlds governed by better standards. Remember, the principle of minimax relative concession entails that some agreements are more rational than others, even if any agreement is better than no agreement at all (Hobbes' view). If we reflect on our moral standards, we will recognize that there is at the very least the **possibility** of alternative moral orders. And "if there are persons whose prospects would be improved by renegotiation, then the existing moral order will be recognizably unstable."[25] From this, Gauthier is led to conclude the following:

> [A]lthough in the real world we begin with an existing
> set of moral principles as constraints on our maximiz-
> ing behaviour, yet we are led by reflection to the idea
> of an amended set that would obtain the agreement of
> everyone and this amended set has, and will be recog-
> nized to have, a stability lacking in existing morality.[26]

In other words, the social contract theory provides us with a means of making moral progress. For instance, when faced with what appears to be a morally arbitrary distinction or principle—e.g., one which bars members of a certain race from employment opportunities—we are able to ask: Are these the constraints upon which rational parties would agree? Do these constraints respect the principle of minimax relative concession? Our rationality allows us all to contemplate these questions. If we do, and if enough of us come to an unfavourable judgment, then the moral standard in question will become "destabilized." This example illustrates a more general point to which Gauthier is led: to the extent that existing moral practices and institutions contravene what people would agree to hypothetically, they will become destabilized, and society will tend to move in the direction of more purely rational moral principles. In this way, then, we can both understand and justify moral progress.

Notes

1. I wish to acknowledge and thank Matthew Barber for his valuable assistance in the preparation of this chapter.

2. For Locke's political theory, see his *Two Treatises of Government* (1690). Hobbes' classic work is *Leviathan* (1651). Rousseau's most influential work was the *Social Contract* (1762). Numerous editions of all three works are in print.

3. Although the sovereign will likely possess physical power with which to enforce obligations, this is not the sense of power meant here. By "empowerment" is meant the granting of Hohfeldian, normative powers to create duties, rights, obligations, and so on. See Chapter 2 above on normative powers.

4. See "Morality, Rational Choice and Semantic Representation" in (eds. E. Paul et al.) *The New Social Contract: Essays on Gauthier* (Blackwell: Oxford, 1988), pp. 173-221. Gauthier is not alone in advocating social contract theory. See also John Rawls' *A Theory of Justice* (London: Oxford University Press, 1971) and T. Scanlon's "Contractualism and Utilitarianism" in *Utilitarianism and Beyond*, eds. A. Sen and B. Williams (Cambridge: Cambridge University Press, 1982).

5. *Ibid.*, 174, emphasis added.

6. The notion of "utility" employed here is a technical term whose meaning will be explored more fully in Chapter 6 below. For now, we can simply understand utility to be a measure of the non-moral value that a person would derive from some particular outcome of some particular action. Of course, many actions have more than one possible outcome, some being more likely than others. And so when we're deciding what to do, we will have to consider not only the various possible outcomes and the utility produced by each outcome, but we will also have to consider, for each possible outcome, the probability that it will (or will not occur). In doing this, we employ a concept philosophers and economists call **expected utility**. Expected utility is a measure which takes into account **probabilities** as well as **utilities**. Suppose there are two actions open to me, and (simplifying matters tremendously) that each one has two possible outcomes. First action: I go with my wife to see a movie that I think I'm going to really like (e.g., *Hannibal*). Here there are two possible outcomes for me. Outcome 1: It is 90% certain that I will derive 100 units of utility (pleasure, desire fulfilment, preference fulfilment, happiness, etc.) from the experience.

But there is another possible outcome: there is a 10% chance that I might in fact be disappointed, and derive only 10 units of utility from the experience. Second action: I instead go to the movie my wife really wants to see (*Love Story*). This action also has, we will suppose, only two possible outcomes: there is a 80% chance that I will personally derive only 10 units of utility. But again, it's remotely possible that I will be surprised and really like my wife's selection. There is a 20% chance that I will in fact derive 70 units of utility. So there are two actions open to me. On the first my expected utility is (100 x 90%) + (10 x 10%) = 91. In other words, taking into account the probabilities and utilities associated with the two possible outcomes of the act, the expected utility of going to see *Hannibal* is 91 units of utility. By going to see *Love Story*, on the other hand, my expected utility is (10 x 80%) + (70 x 20%) = 22.

Leaving aside factors like my wish to please my wife, my desire not to precipitate a divorce, etc., I am better off going to see *Hannibal*. I can expect to derive 91 units of utility from the experience, whereas going to see *Love Story* is likely to result in only 22 units. It goes without saying that my wife's expected utilities would be **very** different indeed.

7. *Leviathan*, Part I, ch. 13.

8. That the theory bases morality in the agreement of **rational** individuals may threaten the moral standing of individuals lacking in "rationality," e.g., infants, some mentally challenged individuals and animals. In the view of some people, this feature of social contract theory is enough to disqualify it as a plausible account of morality.

9. As noted in Chapter 1 above, prudence exclusively concerns the individual agent's own self-interest or well being. The interests of others count only if and to the extent that they impact on those of the agent herself. To act prudently is to act in such a way as to maximize one's own expected utilities.

10. Here we have yet another reason why some insist that social contract theories of morality must be utterly rejected as providing a distorted picture of morality. The latter is, in its very nature, a device for constraining the unbridled pursuit of self-interest. Social contract theorists typically reply that the cultivation of tendencies to observe moral constraints on the pursuit of self-interest is something which, in the long run, actually works to our personal advantage. More on this below, and later when we explore indirect versions of consequentialism in Chapter 6.

11. David Gauthier, *Morals By Agreement* (Oxford: Clarendon, 1986), 178.

12. *Ibid.*, 166.

13. *Ibid.*, 166.

14. Gilbert Harman, "Rationality in Agreement: A Commentary on Gauthier's *Morals By Agreement*" in *The New Social Contract: Essays on Gauthier, supra* note 4, p.2.

15. *Morals By Agreement*, 4.

16. *Ibid.*, 158.

17. *Ibid.*, 168.

18. See, *Ibid.*, 174.

19. *Ibid.*, 183.

20. Think of Hobbes' brutal state of nature compared with the somewhat better world we now inhabit.

21. We will simplify here and talk of utilities, not expected utilities. In other words, we will assume that, for each possible action there is only one possible outcome per person.

22. See *Morals By Agreement*, 142.

23. *Ibid.*, 137.

24. *Ibid.*, 226.

25. "Morality, Rational Choice and Semantic Representation," *supra* note 4, 178.

26. *Ibid.*, 180.

Part II
Normative Ethical Theories

Six
Utilitarianism

Mill and Bentham

The first normative theory we will explore is Utilitarianism. This is a general normative theory which came to prominence in the eighteenth and nineteenth centuries in the writing of Jeremy Bentham and his disciple, John Stuart Mill. Utilitarians rejected both the Divine Command Theory and any appeal to "Natural Law." Bentham is famous for describing the latter as "nonsense on stilts."[1] Utilitarians also reject any form of moral relativism. The principle of utility serves, in their view, as a universal, objective standard for determining, in a rational and systematic way, our moral rights, obligations and duties. It also serves, in the minds of Bentham and Mill, as a powerful tool for assessing the activities of public institutions like courts and legislatures. For utilitarian social reformers like Mill and Bentham all actions, public and private, are open to evaluation on the basis of their utility. Utilitarians have, of course, introduced many modifications to their theory in the years following Mill and Bentham. Some of these will be considered below. But our primary focus will be on Mill and Bentham.

Utilitarian Theories of Value

Utilitarianism is a monistic, consequentialist theory of obligation which, owing to its consequentialist nature, rests on a theory of value.[2] The value of an action always lies in its utility, it's good consequences. But the relevant consequences will vary depending on which theory of value the utilitarian espouses.[3]

A Monistic Theory of Value: Hedonism

The most influential monistic theory of value associated with utilitarianism is **hedonism**, a view which has its roots in Ancient Greek philosophy and was adopted by Bentham and Mill. According to the latter, the only thing of ultimate, irreducible value — of "utility" — is **happiness**, by which was meant **pleasure** and the absence of pain; and the only thing of ultimate, irreducible disvalue — of "disutility" — is unhappiness, which was equated with pain and the absence of pleasure.

> [T]he creed which accepts as the foundation of morals "utility" or "the greatest happiness principle" holds that actions are right in proportion as they tend to promote happiness, wrong as they tend to produce the reverse of happiness. By happiness is intended pleasure, and the absence of pain; by unhappiness, pain and the privation of pleasure.[4]

Food and friendship have utility only because, and to the extent that, their presence produces pleasure and their absence brings pain. Indeed, anything else besides pleasure and the absence of pain is valuable only instrumentally, as a means to the production of pleasure and the absence of pain. This entails, Bentham thought, the following consequence. "Quantity of pleasure being equal, pushpin is as good as poetry."[5] Mill disagreed with this view of pleasure and happiness, preferring instead to say that there are different kinds of happiness and that these can be ranked in terms of their **quality**. Mill is famous for claiming that "it is better to be a human being dissatisfied than a pig satisfied; better to be Socrates dissatisfied than a fool satisfied. And if the fool, or the pig, are of a different opinion, it is because they only know their own side of the question."[6] In other words, the pleasures of the mind are, in Mill's view, of a much higher quality than the "baser" pleasures derived from physical pleasures. It would take a very large amount of the latter to outweigh (in terms of value or utility produced) a tiny amount of the former. What little happiness or pleasure one might derive from reading Shakespeare's plays could not be outweighed by anything but a tremendous amount of pleasure derived from gorging oneself on ice cream. This is because the former is, in Mill's view, of a much higher quality than the latter. How one ranks pleasures in terms of quality, and how one is to compare pleasures of differing quality, are questions Mill never succeeded in answering. Most philosophers believe that this aspect of Mill's theory introduces insurmountable difficulties for him. For how can it be better to be Socrates **dissatisfied** than a pig fully **satisfied**, if the true measure of utility is nothing more than the pleasure and pain our activities produce? Mill's theory of value hints at the idea that pleasure may not be the only thing of ultimate value or utility.[7]

Pluralistic Theories of Value:
G.E. Moore and Preference Utilitarianism

The English philosopher G.E. Moore was, like Mill and Bentham, a utilitarian. But unlike his predecessors Moore espoused a **pluralistic theory of value** which viewed pleasure or happiness as only one of many different things of ultimate, irreducible value. Knowledge and aesthetic experience are, for example, worthy of pursuit for their own sakes. Modern utilitarians tend to take a slightly different tack. Instead of suggesting that we should try to bring about specified states of mind or experiences like knowledge and aesthetic experience, many contemporary utilitarians claim that we should seek to satisfy people's **preferences**, or perhaps their **rational preferences**.[8] Preference utilitarianism is, in principle, more open than Moore's and quite a bit more open than Mill's. It does not specify which objects of preference have utility, and does not restrict us to those which produce pleasure, happiness, aesthetic experiences, and so on. In theory, **any** experience, object, state of affairs—i.e., anything at all—can be the subject of someone's preference. Any (rational) preference can be such that its satisfaction results in the production of utility.

Let's return to Moore. The aesthetic experience of creating or reading a fine piece of literature is, for Moore, not necessarily valuable because of the pleasure it brings us. Indeed, as many creative artists will attest, the production of art is often a highly painful activity. (Think of famously unhappy artists like Van Gogh and Michelangelo.) But it is well worth pursuing because of the valuable aesthetic experiences it is capable of producing, both in the artist herself and in those who are able to experience the fruits of her creativity. Pluralistic theories of value are better able than hedonism to accommodate such features of our experience. But they too encounter serious difficulty: What are we to say about situations where two or more values or valuable things are in competition with each other?[9] If aesthetic experience is a different kind of value than pleasure, how do we compare the two in situations where they conflict? Does there come a point where no amount of aesthetic value can compensate for the emotional pain caused by an artist's activities? At what point (if at all) does the emotional pain caused, in herself, her family and her loved ones, override the value of the aesthetic experiences facilitated by an artist's activities? Is it possible rationally to compare such very different values so as to produce an optimal mix?[10] Is comparing aesthetic experience with pleasure (and pain) too much like comparing apples and oranges?

Monistic Theories Again:
The Problem of Interpersonal Comparisons of Utility

Monistic theories of value may seem preferable on this particular score, but the appearance may be largely illusory. Suppose we are hedonists of the type espoused by Bentham—that is, we see pleasure as the only thing of intrinsic value and are not prepared to complicate things by speaking of different kinds of pleasure somehow ranked in terms of quality. All we have to do is to compare the different **amounts** or **quantities** of pleasure and pain produced by our conduct. This seems to simplify matters considerably: all pleasures and pains can be measured and compared on the same scale. It is perhaps worth noting that we engage, in a rough and ready manner, in such comparisons all the time. I am able to say, with some measure of confidence, that listening to Beethoven's 9th symphony produces in me much more pleasure than listening to Liszt's first piano concerto, which in turn produces significantly more pleasure than listening to Michael Jackson's latest recording. I can make these comparisons even though I cannot be precise about exactly how much I prefer Beethoven to Liszt, and both of these to Michael Jackson. But notice these two points.

First, if we really are going to use something like pleasure and pain as the measure of utility, then we had better have some way of being more precise than I was able to be in the easy example I just used. There will be many situations where I must be able to say, not just that I prefer Beethoven to Liszt, but **how much more** I enjoy Beethoven to Liszt. It is not, however, at all clear how I can do this. Second, and perhaps more importantly, I must not only be able to compare the amounts of pain and pleasure produced within myself, I must also be able to compare the amounts of pleasure and pain produced in me with the amounts produced in everyone else affected by my choices. I must, that is, be able to compare my pleasure with your pleasure, to perform what philosophers and economists call **interpersonal comparisons of utility**. Such comparisons raise serious epistemic difficulties for any consequentialist, including those who hold monistic theories of value. How do I know your mind? How could I possibly quantify and compare your pleasure with my pleasure, your pain with my pain? What scale could we use? We can compare the temperature of one object with that of another because we have things like thermometers. But there seems no comparable device to measure amounts of pleasure and pain produced in different people. And if there is no such device, then how are we to compare the amount of pleasure Sari gets from seeing *The French Lieutenant's Woman* with the pleasure Howie gets from seeing *Terminator*?[11] In some cases, we just seem to know, using "common sense," that one person derives much greater pleasure than another does. It might just be obvious that Sari wants to see *The French Lieutenant's Woman* so very **much more** than Howie wants to see *Terminator*. We might know this, for example, because Sari is willing to give up a lot more to ensure that they see *The French Lieutenant's Woman*. But such cases are no doubt the exception. Often the consequences of our conduct are far reaching and complex and involve many different people of very different characters and dispositions. How do we compare the pleasures of Pope John Paul II with those of Mick Jagger? How do I compare the pleasures and pains caused by a policy forbidding surrogate motherhood, or by my failure to observe a promise to my children? It is often very difficult, then, to assess the various amounts of pleasure and pain produced by our choices. And without a device for systematically measuring pain and pleasure—or whatever states or experiences are thought to be of value or disvalue—the problem of interpersonal comparison looms large for any kind of consequentialist theory, including utilitarianism.

Theories of Obligation: Act Utilitarianism

When we turn to the utilitarian's theories of obligation, we discover that there are essentially two different kinds: act and rule utilitarianism.[12] Act utilitarianism (AU) defines the rightness or wrongness of individual actions in terms of the good or bad consequences realized by those actions themselves. In other words, AU defines the rightness or wrongness of an action in terms of **its** utility and disutility. Again, the term "utility" stands for whatever it is that is intrinsically valuable under the utilitarian's theory of value, "disutility" for whatever is thought to be intrinsically bad. According to Mill, "actions are right in proportion as they tend to promote happiness; wrong as they tend to produce the reverse of happiness."[13] As we saw, for Mill "utility" means happiness, and "disutility" unhappiness. And by "happiness" he means pleasure and the absence of pain; and by "unhappiness" he means pain and the absence of pleasure. But as we also saw, a utilitarian need not make this identification, nor need he define utility in terms of happiness. Regardless of the theory of value with which it is associated, however, AU always makes the following claim:

> AU: An act is right if and only if there is no other action I could have done instead which either (a) would have produced a greater balance of utility over disutility; or (b) would have produced a smaller balance of disutility over utility.

We must add (b) to account for those unfortunate situations where whatever we do we seem to cause more disutility than utility—where we're damned if we do and damned if we don't. In short, AU tells us to act always so as to bring about the best consequences we can, and sometimes that means trying to make the best of a bad situation.

AU was made famous in the early modern period by Mill and Bentham, at a time when it was quite natural for many people to think that some individuals simply count more than others do. There were some who thought that members of the aristocracy, the Church, or a particular race were morally superior to others and were therefore deserving of special consideration or privilege. The utilitarians were part of a social revolution which would have none of this. In the famous words of Bentham, "each is to count for one, none to count for more than one." In other words, according to utilitarians, **all** those affected by my actions should count

equally in my deliberations concerning my moral obligations. The happiness of the king is to count equally with the equal happiness of the shop clerk. Mill put this important point in the following way:

> I must again repeat what the assailants of utilitarianism seldom have the justice to acknowledge, that the happiness which forms the utilitarian standard of what is right in conduct is **not** the agent's own happiness but that of all concerned. As between others, utilitarianism requires him to be as **strictly impartial as a disinterested benevolent spectator.**[14]

So built into AU is a commitment to equality and impartiality. We are to be concerned equally and impartially with the utility of everyone, including ourselves, who might be affected by our actions. On these grounds alone AU is a very appealing theory. What could be better than to be sure that I always maximize, not my own happiness or that of my friends, but the happiness of all those people affected by my actions whoever they might be? What more could morality require? Despite its inherently desirable features, many philosophers have come to find serious difficulties with AU. These have led some utilitarians to opt for alternative forms of the theory.

Difficulties for Act Utilitarianism

Special Relationships

One of the more serious difficulties for AU involves **special relationships**. These latter include relationships we have with our family members, friends, colleagues, patients, clients, and so on. Such special relationships are thought by many to require some degree of partiality and special concern towards others. It would be wrong, some think, to be impartial between friends and family on the one hand and perfect strangers on the other. It would be equally wrong to be impartial between one's patient and the many others who might benefit from the knowledge to be gained from using one's patient in a medical experiment. The importance of personal relationships in the moral evaluation of conduct is often stressed by feminists who reject the "impartiality" required by utilitarianism. In their view, treating everyone the same would be equivalent to treating all of them as strangers. And how could this possibly be the right thing to do?[15]

Here's a simple case which illustrates the concern of those who view special relationships as posing a difficulty for AU. Suppose that my children want new clothes to begin the school year. The clothes they already have are more than adequate, but in the past they have derived a certain amount of happiness from beginning the school year with a new set of threads. There is no reason to think that they have changed in this regard. Down the street lives a widowed, unemployed father, Tom, and his two children. The children have nothing but somewhat tattered summer clothes, and Tom lacks the financial resources to buy new clothing. Furthermore, the three lack the support of an extended family and are ineligible for government assistance. AU would seem to require that I forgo buying my kids their new clothes so that I can give the money to Tom. My children can make do with their perfectly acceptable clothes, but the utility they would derive from their new clothes would be vastly outweighed by the increase in happiness experienced by Tom's kids were he able to use the money to buy them new clothes instead. But is this right? Must I be **impartial** between the happiness of my children and that of Tom's? Many think not, and therefore reject AU as the sole basis for our moral obligations. It neglects the special duties I owe my children and all the many others with whom I share a special relationship.

Past Actions and Moral Commitments

Another related objection to AU is its apparent failure to account for moral commitments and the rights they generate. AU is a forward-looking theory. That is, it requires that we act so as to maximize the utility which lies in **future** consequences. What occurred in the past is relevant, according to AU, only to the extent that it has some bearing on what might occur in the future. But according to many people, past actions and commitments sometimes determine what we ought to do now. In other words, moral reasons are often **backward-looking**. A promise made can serve as a moral reason for action now, even though it occurred in the past. It can create moral rights and corresponding duties. Consider the following example.

Suppose your good friend, Monica, informs you that she has a very serious illness. Your friendship with Monica goes a long way back and is immensely important to you both. After telling you the sad news, Monica has you promise that you will mention nothing to her husband, Jack. You know Jack only slightly, but you also know very well that he and Monica are extremely close and that he would be devastated were he to find out later that Monica's illness had been kept from him. Despite all this, you reckon that a promise is a promise, and that Jack must be left uninformed. Monica has a right that you not tell Jack, and you therefore are under obligation not to do so.

Upon further reflection, however, you begin to wonder whether your moral obligation does ultimately lie in keeping your promise. You add up the utilities and disutilities involved for everyone affected by your decision. The affected individuals include not only Jack and Monica—and you—but their two young children as well. You conclude that overall utility would be maximized, on balance, if you told Jack about Monica's illness. Although she prefers that Jack not be told, and although she would feel angry and betrayed by your action, Monica would derive much greater comfort and support from Jack, who would in turn be able to help the children cope with their mother's medical condition. As a consequence of your valid, act-utilitarian reasoning, you break your promise. You consider it your moral obligation to maximize utility, even at the expense of violating the trust placed in you by your dear friend. It is your duty to break your commitment and violate Monica's rights. But can this be right? According to many critics of AU this cannot be right, and AU must therefore be rejected.

Free Riders and the Duty of Fair Play

So promises and other such special commitments pose difficulties for AU. Free riders do too. Suppose there is a temporary but serious energy shortage in your community. All private homes and businesses have been requested to conserve electricity and gas. Private homes are to keep their thermostats no higher than 15 degrees centigrade and all businesses are temporarily to cut production by one-half. If everyone helps out in this way a serious overload which would prove disastrous will be avoided. Being a good act utilitarian, and knowing the tendencies of your neighbours, you reason as follows.

I know that everyone else will pay scrupulous attention to the government's request. So the potential disaster will be averted regardless of what I do. It will make no difference whatsoever if I run my production lines at two-thirds capacity. The little bit of extra electricity we use will have no negative effect at all. Of course if everyone ran at two-thirds, then disaster would result. But I know this is not going to happen and so the point is irrelevant. As for my employees, they will see a reduction and assume that the cut was to one-half, so no one will know but me. Using two-thirds, then, will in no way prove harmful, but it will make a considerable amount of difference to my balance sheet. The extra production will enable the company to show a much higher profit this year. All things considered, then, it is morally permissible, indeed, it's my moral obligation, to run at two-thirds. This is what AU tells me that I should do.

Imagine the moral outrage that would ensue were your acting on this line of reasoning to become common knowledge. If the case seems far-fetched, consider how an analogous line of reasoning could be employed to justify extra diagnostic tests for a patient, or to justify putting pesticides on your lawn while your neighbours all voluntarily pursue more environmentally friendly practices. Were you to pursue these lines of conduct, you would be labelled a "free rider," one who rides freely while others shoulder the burdens necessary for all to prosper. Your actions would be thought to violate a **duty of fair play** owed to all those who willingly sacrifice their best interests, or the interests of those placed in their care, for the good of everyone concerned. All this despite your efforts to maximize the utility of your actions.

Act and Consequence: The Importance of Intentions

AU claims that the moral status of my conduct is determined by its future consequences alone, by the extent to which it produces utility and disutility. The very nature of the act is irrelevant. That it amounts to the breaking of a promise or is patently unfair are, in themselves, neither here nor there. All that matters are the good or bad consequences of whatever it is that I choose to do. Yet many people think that the **intentions** with which an action are carried out can have a profound bearing on its moral status. Consider, once again, a scenario outlined in Chapter 2 above: the President's momentous decision whether to bring down a hijacked airliner destined to crash into a densely populated office building.

It is reasonably easy to see how a simple AU approach, which directs us to maximize the utility of our actions, might lead to the conclusion that the President should order the military to destroy the jet. Many innocent lives—and all the utility associated with them—will either be lost or profoundly affected for the worse by this military action. But thousands more will be similarly affected if the action is not taken, thus leading to the difficult, though inescapable, conclusion that the jet must be brought down. If our moral obligation is always, in every situation in which we are called on to act, to maximize the good and minimize the bad consequences of what we do, there may be no other option open to the President.

Yet many people will object to this line of reasoning, suggesting that there is a morally relevant feature of the President's dilemma which is completely ignored by this simple utilitarian line of thinking. There is, it will be said, a vital difference between the following two courses of conduct:

a. Intentionally bringing about, through one's own conduct and at one's own hand, the death of innocent people.

and

b. Intentionally choosing not to prevent someone else from bringing about, through his actions and at his own hand, the death of innocent people.

According to many thoughtful people, option **b** just might be the morally right course of action. This is so, they will add, even though the foreseeable consequences of that choice include the death of thousands more innocent people. The consequences of **b** may be far worse in terms of utility than the consequences of **a**, but there is more to the moral assessment of actions than considerations of utility. Sometimes the very **nature** of the act, or the **intentions** with which it is performed, can make an important difference. It matters **how** consequences are brought about: it matters whether we bring them about ourselves, or whether they are produced by others whom we might have prevented from acting. In other words, **intentionally** bringing about bad consequences is not equivalent to **foreseeing** that bad consequences will follow one's deliberate choice not to act, a point which is ignored entirely if we restrict ourselves to toting up consequences.

Act Utilitarianism and Supererogation

AU requires that we always maximize the balance of utility over disutility in our actions. If doing X instead of Y will yield a better balance of utility over disutility, then I must do X. Some philosophers are convinced that this theory requires far too much of us. Take again the case of my children and their new school clothes. More utility would be produced were I to give the money to Tom. His children would derive much more utility from this donation than my better off children could ever derive from their new clothes. But there is another alternative which has yet to be considered. There are many starving children in the world who are in desperate need of food, clothing and other necessities of life. The $300 Tom or I could spend on our children's clothing would produce far more utility were the money donated to Oxfam instead. The $300 dollars might actually save a life, or at the very least rescue many people from impoverished lives of despair and starvation. In other words, donating my $300 to Oxfam would produce a good deal more utility than either of the two options with which I began. So AU tells me that I should donate the money instead of putting it towards new school clothes.

Fair enough. But now comes a further consequence which troubles those who view AU as a plausible moral theory. The example just considered is easily generalized. If my $300 will produce so much more utility if I donate it to charity rather than spend it on my children, then can the same not be said for all my financial resources over and above those necessary to maintain a minimum level of comfort and well being? Suppose I make $50,000 per year. Suppose further that my family can live a very comfortable, but modest, existence on $25,000. I would not be able to afford a car, but we can take public transit. I could not afford a house, but we can live in a comfortable three bedroom rental unit. My children will not have the latest "designer" clothes, but they can easily make do with less expensive clothing. Etc. If AU is correct, then it would seem that I should donate at least half my income to charity! My family and I may lose out on all the utility that we could gain from the extra $25,000, but this would be more than compensated for by the vastly greater amounts of utility that money could be used to produce. How, after all, does one compare the disappointment of not having designer clothes with the pain of going to bed each night cold and hungry?

Most people believe that we have a moral duty to help those in need of our charity, or of other forms of assistance. But most people also believe that this duty does not extend as far as the reasoning of the last paragraph would suggest. We should be charitable, but not to the extent that we are reduced to a point just above the level of abject poverty. There is, most think, a difference between conduct which is morally **required** or **obligatory**—like giving some measure of support to charity—and that which, though morally commendable and praiseworthy, lies beyond the call of moral duty. In Chapter 2 we called such conduct "acts of **supererogation**." AU seems to draw no such distinction, however. If I am to maximize the balance of utility over disutility, then it would seem that I am **always** under **obligation** to divest myself of whatever resources might be put to better use by someone else. This, however, seems to require too much.

The Act Utilitarian Replies: Long-Range, Indirect Consequences

Despite its apparent weaknesses, AU remains the preferred theory of many utilitarians. How, then, can the above objections be answered? The first move a defender of AU will likely make is to suggest that the critics have in each instance failed to consider **all** the relevant consequences. Take the example of Monica and Jack. Of crucial importance is not simply the fact that Monica and her family will probably fare

The Dimensions of Ethics

better if Jack is informed, but also **(1)** that your action will almost certainly destroy at least one valuable relationship (your friendship with Monica) which, in the long run, would add significantly to the utility you are able to bring about in future actions. **(2)** It might also weaken, perhaps even undermine, an important character trait the inculcation of which in yourself helps ensure that you always do the right thing in situations where you might be tempted to do otherwise. In most situations, keeping one's promise produces the most utility. Yet it is often tempting to break our promise to secure an advantage for ourselves or someone close to us. A firmly entrenched tendency **always** to keep one's promises is an indispensable means of rendering it unlikely that one will not give in to such temptation. That tendency will be threatened if you break your promise to Monica. **(3)** There is also the possibility that your betrayal will become common knowledge, thus threatening your status as a friend who can be trusted. Without the trust of your friends and family, how can you derive any benefits from these immensely valuable relationships? If you cannot be trusted to maintain confidences, your friends will stop treating you as one worthy of the trust essential to **any** special relationship. Of course **(4)** there is also the possibility that your actions will lead your friends and family to mistrust other people as well—an even more disastrous possibility, viewed from the perspective of AU. All of these **long-range, indirect** consequences of breaking your promise to Monica, when put into the balance, tip the scales in favour of keeping your word. Similar things can always be said, the defender of AU will reply, to account for special relationships, moral commitments, duties of fair play, the distinction between required acts and acts of supererogation, and so on. Those who think that AU fails to take such factors seriously have simply ignored all the long-range, indirect effects of doing so.[16]

Desert Islands: The Critic Strikes Back

So the defender of AU has fairly forceful replies to many objections to his theory of obligation. When a critic provides such objections, we should always be sure to ask: Have all the relevant consequences, long-range and indirect as well as immediate and direct, been accounted for? In all likelihood, they have not. This is true whether we are talking about breaking promises or confidences, violating someone's autonomy, free riding, or performing acts of charity which seem supererogatory.

Philosophers are fairly industrious when it comes to thinking up counter-examples to ethical theories. Having met replies such as the above, they have altered their counter examples to get rid of those convenient indirect, long-range effects upon which the above defence of AU was based. One such example is the **Desert Island Promise Case**, a version of which now follows.

You and a friend are alone on a deserted island. Your friend is dying and asks you to see to it when you are rescued that the elder of his two sons receives the huge sum of money your friend has secretly stashed away. You now are the only other person who knows of its existence. You solemnly promise to fulfil your friend's final request and he passes away secure in the knowledge that his last wish is in good hands. Upon rescue you are faced with a dilemma. The elder son turns out to be a lazy lout who squanders to no good end—even his own pleasure—whatever money he has. Even when he has lots of money to spend he still ends up being miserable and causing misery to other people. Your friend's younger son, however, is an aspiring researcher in dermatology. He is on the brink of uncovering a solution to the heartache of psoriasis, but will fail unless he receives financial backing. All his applications for grants have unjustly been denied and he has been left in desperation. As a good act utilitarian, you reason that utility would obviously be maximized if your solemn word to your dying friend were broken and you gave the money to the younger son. Think of all the utility that would be realized, all the suffering that would be alleviated! Compare this with the very little utility and considerable disutility that would result were you to give the money to the elder son.

Notice that in this case most of the indirect, long-range consequences to which appeal was made in Monica's case are absent. No one will know that the promise is being broken—except you of course—and there are no valuable, utility-enhancing relationships in jeopardy.[17] Your friend is dead. There seems little doubt in this situation that the promise should be broken according to AU—this is your moral obligation. But surely, the opponent will argue, this cannot be so.

In response to these (and similar) objections, many utilitarians have responded with the charge that "desert island" scenarios are really quite irrelevant. Moral theories are intended to deal with the kinds of situations we typically encounter in our everyday lives. In these scenarios, the long-range and indirect consequences conveniently eliminated in the desert island case **are** present, and so we need not worry about what AU might require in such an imaginary case. Though this response has some degree of force, there remains the nagging suspicion that the desert island case reveals a fundamental flaw in AU. Even if it gets the right results in everyday cases—e.g., one should almost always keep one's promises—it may get them in the wrong way. As the desert island case illustrates, a promise should (exceptional cases aside) always be kept, not because of the good consequences of doing so, long-range or otherwise, but because of the **kind of act that it is**. The reason you should keep your promise to Monica is not the utility such an action will produce, but because keeping your word to a friend is something valuable in and of itself. The same goes for fairness and the keeping of one's commitments. AU might get the right results in all such cases, but it is far from clear that it gets them in the right way.

Rule Utilitarianism

Seeing the force of the various objections made to it, some utilitarians have developed an alternative to AU. Consider further what would be said if it came to light that you had been "free riding" on the willingness of others to restrict their electricity consumption or prescribe diagnostic tests according to accepted guidelines. The likely response would be to say: "Sure, no utility is lost if you use the extra electricity or prescribe the extra diagnostic tests. But imagine what would happen if everyone did what you are doing. Imagine if that became the norm. Disaster would result!" This request: "Imagine what would happen if everybody did that" has great probative force for many people. If **not everyone** could do what I propose to do without great disutility resulting, then many are prepared to say that it would be wrong for **anyone** to do it, and hence wrong for me to do it. Feeling the force of this intuition, some utilitarians have developed a very different variety of their theory called **rule utilitarianism** (RU). On this version the rightness or wrongness of an action is not judged by its consequences. Rather it is to be judged by the consequences of everyone's adopting a **general rule** under which the action falls.

As an introduction to RU consider a case outlined by John Rawls in his famous paper "Two Concepts of Rules."[18] Rawls has us imagine that we are a sheriff in the deep American south. The rape of a white woman has taken place and although the identity of the rapist is unknown, it is clear that the offender was black. The predominantly white and racially bigoted community is extremely agitated over the incident and great social unrest is threatening. Riots are about to break out and many innocent, and possibly some not so innocent, people will be killed. If you were able to identify and arrest the rapist, the unrest would undoubtedly subside; but unfortunately you have no leads, other than the fact that the rapist was black. It occurs to you that you do not really need the actual culprit to calm things down. Why not simply concoct a case against a randomly chosen black man who has no alibi and have him arrested? The crowd will be placated, and although one innocent man will suffer, many innocent lives will be saved.

Rawls uses this example to illustrate an apparent weakness in AU and how RU allows one to overcome it. The consequences of framing the (possibly) innocent black are far better (or less bad), in terms of utility, than allowing the riot to occur. Hence AU seems to require the frame—a course of action which is clearly unjust—and a violation of the innocent black man's rights. Of course the defender of AU has several tricks up his sleeve at this point. He can once again appeal to the possible indirect effects of the frame.

Suppose the lie came to light. Terrible social paranoia and unrest would result; people would no longer trust the judicial system and would wonder constantly whether they might be next. Indirect consequences such as these, the defender of AU will argue, clearly outweigh any short-term, direct benefits. But Rawls suggests that we consider a different question than the one AU would have us ask. We are to consider whether a general rule which permits the framing of innocent persons could possibly figure in a moral code whose general acceptance would result in the maximization of utility. If it could not (which is surely the case), then the proposed frame is morally impermissible. Since no such general rule could find its way into an acceptable moral code, largely for the reasons mentioned above, an action in accordance with that rule would be morally wrong. Hence it would be morally wrong on RU to frame the possibly innocent black, even if the consequences of that particular action would be better than those of the alternatives. We are not morally required, on RU, to perform actions which individually would maximize utility. Rather we are to perform actions which accord with a set of rules whose general observance would maximize utility. Actions are judged according to whether they conform with acceptable rules; only the rules themselves are judged in terms of utility. The essence of RU is expressed in the following claim:

> RU: An act is morally right if and only if it conforms with a set of rules whose general observance would maximize utility.

One extremely important difference between RU and AU is worth stressing. It is quite possible, on RU, to be required to perform an action which does not, on that particular occasion, maximize utility. Observance of the best set of general rules does not, on each individual occasion, always lead to the best consequences. Of course it **generally** does, but there are exceptions. This is something the defender of RU seems willing to live with for the sake of overall, long-term utility gains and the ability to deal with desert-island promises, free riders, and so on.

Rule Utilitarianism: Rule Worship?

RU is not without its difficulties. Some critics claim, for example, that RU really does violate the spirit of utilitarianism and amounts to "rule worship."[19] If the ideal behind utilitarianism is the maximization of utility, then should we not be able to deviate from the generally acceptable rules when doing so will clearly serve to maximize utility? If the defender of RU allows exceptions to be made in such cases, then he runs the risk of collapsing his RU into AU. The rules will no longer hold any special weight or authority in our moral decisions. We will end up following the rules when it is best to do so and depart from them when that seems best.[20] In each case we seem led to do what AU requires, namely, maximize the utility of our individual actions. If, on the other hand, the defender of RU holds fast and says we must **never** deviate from rules which generally advance utility but sometimes do not, then the charge of rule worship comes back to plague the utilitarian.

Ideal Codes for a Non-Ideal World

A second major problem facing RU can be summed up in an example. Suppose it were true that the best set of rules for the circumstances of our society place an obligation on first-born children to provide for their elderly parents. I, the younger of

two sons, reason that I therefore have no obligation whatsoever to provide for my elderly parents, even though I know
that my elder brother is unwilling to provide more than the
50 per cent he thinks we each ought to provide. My parents
end up living a life of abject poverty on only 50 per cent
of what they need to sustain themselves. Something seems
clearly wrong here. Our obligations, it would seem, cannot
be entirely a function of an **ideal code** which may never in
fact be followed by anyone except me. We seem to require, in
an acceptable moral theory, some recognition of how other
people are behaving, what rules they are in fact following.
The rules they are following may be perfectly acceptable but
not ideal, in which case I should perhaps follow them too.
Perhaps here the excuse, "But no one else is willing to do it"
carries some weight.

The Right Answers for the Wrong Reason

As we saw above, a common objection to AU is that in many
cases it provides the right answer but the wrong reason. The
reason we should (normally) keep our promises is not that
the consequences of doing so, short and long term, direct
and indirect, are better if we do so. The reason we should,
exceptional cases aside, keep our promises is that keeping a
promise is, in itself, the morally right thing to do. An analogous complaint is sometimes made against RU. Here too
the nagging suspicion remains that it might get the right results—we should almost always observe a rule requiring the
keeping of promises, always observe general rules of fair play,
and so on—but for the wrong reasons. As the desert island
case illustrates, perhaps a promise should (exceptional cases
aside) always be kept, not because general observance of a
rule requiring this conduct will serve to maximize utility but

because of the **kind of act** that it singles out. The same goes for rules about fairness, the keeping of one's special commitments to one's children, and so on. Like AU, RU might get the right results in most cases, but it is far from clear that it gets them in the right way.

Notes

1. Jeremy Bentham, *Anarchical Fallacies*, in Volume Two of *The Works of Jeremy Bentham*, ed. John Bowring (New York: 1962), 500. Although Bentham's target was any theory which claims that there is a natural law which establishes "imprescriptible" natural rights, his specific target was the Declaration of the Rights of Man of the French National Assembly (1791). He thought such doctrines were not only "nonsense on stilts" but "terrorist language" as well. It is perhaps important to add that, Bentham notwithstanding, Utilitarianism is compatible, in principle, with the various bases for morality discussed in Part I above. It is possible that the Principle of Utility is: commanded by God, the fundamental maxim of the Natural Law, or the principle upon which rational contractors would settle. It might even be true that our culture has adopted, as its foundational moral standard, the principle of utility. So Utilitarianism may even be compatible with Moral Relativism.

2. These terms are introduced and defined in Chapter 2 above.

3. The term "utilitarianism" is sometimes reserved for theories, such as Bentham's and Mill's, which restrict the relevant consequences to "happiness" or even "pleasure." Those so-called utilitarians who reject hedonism will be thought of as espousing non-utilitarian brands of **consequentialism**. In this book, we will adopt the wider understanding of the term "utilitarianism" since many historically influential — and self-described — utilitarians are happy to couch their theories in terms of, e.g., preference satisfaction or other non-reducible values like friendship and knowledge. See, e.g., the writings of G.E. Moore, whose views are discussed below. See also R.M. Hare's *Moral Thinking* (Oxford: Oxford University Press, 1981).

4. John Stuart Mill, *Utilitarianism*, (New York: Bobbs Merrill, 1957), 10.

5. Bentham, *An Introduction to the Principles of Morals and Legislation* (1789) in *The Works of Jeremy Bentham*, *supra* note 1. Pushpin was a rather mindless, children's game.

Six :: *Utilitarianism*

6. Mill, *Utilitarianism*, 16.

7. Mill has here been presented as suggesting that higher pleasures are higher because a small amount of higher pleasure is equivalent to a large amount of lower pleasure. This is an admittedly controversial reading of Mill. In introducing his test of quality, Mill writes: "If one of the two [pleasures] is, by those who are competently acquainted with both, placed so far above the other that ... they would not resign it for **any quantity** of the other pleasure which their nature is capable of, we are justified in ascribing to the preferred enjoyment a superiority in quality..." (*Utilitarianism*, 16, emphasis added.) This suggests that for Mill the value of higher pleasures may be in principle prior to that of lower pleasures so that **no** amount of the latter could possibly compensate for the former. This seems implausible, however, and so we are perhaps better off ascribing to Mill the weaker position according to which a very large amount of lower pleasure could compensate for a very small amount of the "higher" pleasures.

8. Some of our preferences may not be rational—e.g., those based on false beliefs. And some of our rational preferences—e.g., those we would have were we fully informed and thinking clearly—may not be ones we actually have. Whether we should maximize actual or rational preferences is a question which divides modern utilitarians. On why we focus on rational preferences see, e.g., R.M. Hare's *Moral Thinking*.

9. Preference utilitarianism shares with Moore's view many of its advantages and disadvantages. For example, how is one to rank preferences for such widely different things as ice cream and Mozart? Or how is one to rank Jackie's preference for Mozart as compared with Josh's preference for The Bare Naked Ladies?

10. Again, similar questions arise if we are talking about the satisfaction of actual or rational preferences.

11. This case was discussed earlier in Chapter 5.

12. A similar distinction is sometimes drawn between "direct" and "indirect" consequentialism. (It is important to remember that utilitarianism is not, strictly speaking, the only form of consequentialist theory. Not all consequentialists employ the concept of "utility," preferring instead to talk of the good and bad consequences of our actions. This is partly because the term "utility" is often associated with hedonism and not all consequentialists are hedonists.) Some consequentialists, including those who call themselves utilitarians, prefer not to restrict themselves to asking about the utility of (or consequences of adopting) **rules**. Some, such as R.M. Hare, ask which **principles** and **traits of**

character are such that their adoption and inculcation will, in the long run, maximize utility. Since we aim at maximizing utility **through** adopting certain principles and character traits, the goal of performing actions which lead to the greatest utility (or best consequences) is pursued indirectly. Hence a theory which instructs us to do so is called "indirect consequentialism." On the other hand, a theory which tells us to determine, on each and every occasion, which **action** will maximize utility (or achieve the best consequences) instructs us to aim directly at good consequences. Such a theory will therefore be considered a form of "direct consequentialism." In this chapter we will restrict ourselves to speaking in terms of utility and in terms of the differences between act and rule utilitarianism, with the understanding that much of what is said applies to most forms of indirect and direct consequentialism. For Hare's indirect consequentialist theory, see *Moral Thinking*.

13. Mill, *Utilitarianism*, 10.

14. *Ibid.*, 22.

15. See Chapter 10 below.

16. For a sustained defence of a kind of AU which places great emphasis on long-range, indirect consequences of our conduct upon ourselves and others, see Hare's *Moral Thinking*. Hare splits moral thinking into two levels. First, there is the "intuitive level" where we adopt character traits and follow general principles the inculcation of which in ourselves and others will maximize utility. This is the level we are to utilize in everyday life, except when a serious anomaly or moral dilemma causes us to question our intuitive level principles. Then there is the "critical level," to which we must ascend when choosing, critiquing or clarifying the commitments of our intuitive level principles. At this level we are to follow the dictates of a kind of AU which seeks the maximization of rational preferences.

17. Your own tendency to keep promises may, of course, be threatened since **you** know what you intend to do. But given the highly unusual nature of the situation, and the fact that it represents an isolated incident, there is reason to think that your own moral resolve will not be seriously threatened.

18. John Rawls, "Two Concepts of Rules," in *The Philosophical Review*, January, 1955.

19. See J.J.C. Smart and Bernard Williams, *Utilitarianism: For and Against* (London: Cambridge University Press, 1973), 10.

20. See David Lyons, *The Forms and Limits of Utilitarianism* (Oxford: Oxford University Press, 1965) where it is argued that any version of RU faithful to the utilitarian credo collapses logically into AU.

Seven

The Deontological Ethics
of Immanuel Kant

Reason and Morality

Immanuel Kant was a German philosopher renowned for
his revolutionary metaphysical and epistemological theories, and for his very strict deontological moral theory. The
latter stressed the absolute or "exceptionless" nature of
moral rules, together with the irrelevance of consequences
or feelings in the assessment of moral judgments. As a strong
deontologist Kant was opposed to all forms of consequentialism. He was also opposed to any type of non-cognitiv-
ism in ethical theory, particularly the form espoused by the
eighteenth-century Scottish philosopher, David Hume, who
viewed moral judgments as expressions of a special kind of
"moral sense" or "sentiment."[1] According to Kant, morality
is not concerned with expressing our feelings. Nor is it a matter of maximizing consequences like pleasure and happiness.
On the contrary, the basis for morality is **reason**. It is our
capacity to deliberate about, and act upon, valid reasons for
action which makes us moral beings. In discerning the requirements of right reason we are guided by what Kant called

the **Categorical Imperative**, the fundamental principle of Kant's moral theory, and the fundamental basis for all of our moral judgments.

A Monistic Theory of Obligation

Kant, like Mill, proposes a monistic theory of obligation. But unlike Mill, Kant denies that the consequences of our actions have anything at all to do with their rightness or wrongness. According to Kant,

> An action done from duty has its moral worth, not in **the purpose** [i.e., the consequences] to be attained by it, but in the maxim in accordance with which it is decided upon; it depends, therefore, not on the realization of the object of the action, but solely on the **principle of volition** [the maxim] in accordance with which, irrespective of all objects of the faculty of desire [i.e., pleasure, happiness, preferences] the action has been performed.[2]

In this remark we see clearly that Kant espouses a strong deontological theory of obligation which rejects all appeal to consequences. The morality of an action is determined not by its consequences but by the maxim, the general principle, to which it conforms. Its moral worth lies not in the happiness or pleasure it produces, i.e., its utility, but in the kind of action it is. Let's try to clarify this point.

Maxims

A key notion in Kant's moral theory is the notion of a maxim. By this technical term Kant means a general rule or principle which specifies (a) what it is I conceive myself as doing; and (b) my reason for doing it. For example, suppose I decide to tell a lie in order to avoid distress to my friend. The maxim of my action could be expressed in the following way: "Whenever I am able to avoid distress to my friend by lying, I shall do so." This maxim makes plain that I conceive myself as lying and that my reason is the avoidance of my friend's distress. It makes plain that I consider the avoidance of such distress as a **sufficient reason** to lie. Were I to act on my maxim I would in effect be expressing my commitment to a universal rule of action which extends in its scope beyond the particular situation in which I find myself. In supposing that the avoidance of my friend's distress is a sufficient reason in that situation to lie, I commit myself to holding that in **any** other situation just like it, i.e., any other case in which a lie would serve to avoid a friend's distress, I should tell a lie. This **universalizability of reasons** and maxims can perhaps be illustrated through an example involving a non-moral judgment.

Suppose you and I are baseball fans.

I say to you, "The Toronto Blue Jays are a good baseball team because their team batting average is about .260 and the average ERA among their starting pitchers is under 3.50."

You reply, "What is your opinion of the Boston Red Sox?"

I say, "They are a lousy team."

You reply, "But their team batting average is also about .260 and the average ERA among their starters is 3.40."

I am stuck here in a logical inconsistency. I must either modify my earlier assessment of the Blue Jays—say that they too are a lousy team—or admit that the Red Sox are also a good team. By citing my reasons for judging the Blue Jays a good ball team, I commit myself to a universalized maxim that **any** baseball team with a team batting average of over .260 and whose starting rotation has an ERA of below 3.50 is a good baseball team. If I don't agree with the implications of that universalized maxim, e.g., I still think the Red Sox are a bad ball team, then logical consistency demands that I reject or modify the maxim. Perhaps I will add that in addition to a team batting average of over .260 and a ERA among starting pitchers of under 3.50, a good baseball team must have several "clutch" players. I would add this if I thought that the absence of clutch players explains why the Red Sox, unlike the Blue Jays, are not a good team. Of course I could make this alteration only if I thought the Blue Jays did have at least a few clutch players.

So my maxim that whenever I can avoid distress to my friend by lying I shall do so, insofar as it expresses a general reason for action, applies to other situations similar to the one in which I initially act upon it. But this is not the full extent of my commitment. If avoiding a friend's distress really is a sufficient reason for **my** telling a lie, then it must also be a sufficient reason for **anyone else** who finds herself in a situation just like mine. According to Kant, and virtually all moral philosophers, acting upon a maxim commits me, as a rational moral agent, to a **universal moral rule or principle** governing all persons in situations just like mine (in the relevant respects). I must be prepared to accept that a sufficient reason for me is a sufficient reason for anyone else in precisely my situation. This is the force of the first formulation of Kant's Categorical Imperative we are about to consider. If I think some other person in a position to avoid a friend's distress by lying should not tell the lie, then I must either retract my earlier maxim or specify some relevant difference between our situations, as I did when I tried to show that the Red Sox are a bad baseball team despite their strong team batting average and pitching staff.

The Categorical Imperative I: Universalizability

Acting for reasons, that is, acting rationally (which is required, according to Kant if we are to be moral), commits me to universal rules or maxims which I must be prepared to accept. Kant expresses this point in terms of my capacity to will that my personal maxim should become a **universal law**. According to this first formulation of the Categorical Imperative, the fundamental principle of obligation in Kant's monistic system is: "I ought never to act except in such a way that **I can also will that my maxim should become a universal law.**"[3] Later he writes, "**Act as if the maxim of your action were to become through your will a universal law of nature.**"[4] According to Kant, immoral maxims and the immoral actions based upon them can never, under any conceivable circumstances, pass the Categorical Imperative test. This is not, as we shall now see, because the consequences of general observance of an immoral maxim would be undesirable in terms of utility. (That's the rule utilitarian explanation.) Rather it is because the state of affairs in which the maxim is observed as a universal law is in some way contradictory or logically inconsistent.

Logical Consistency and Acting on Reasons

Some things or states of affairs simply cannot exist, in the strongest sense of "cannot." This is the sense of the word "cannot" we use when we say that there cannot be a square circle, or that 2 + 3 can never equal 6. We say that such scenarios are **logically impossible**—we violate the rules of logical thinking if we suppose that they could possibly exist. The state of affairs in which I am, at one and the same time, Rob's father **and** Rob's son is in this sense logically impossible. It simply cannot exist. Were I for some strange reason to will—i.e., choose to bring about—that this state of affairs should exist, my will, Kant would say, would contradict itself. It would be willing a logically inconsistent state of affairs: that I am Rob's father and son at one and the same time. Now consider a case actually discussed by Kant. Suppose that a man

> finds himself driven to borrowing money because of need. He well knows that he will not be able to pay it back; but he sees too that he will get no loan unless he gives a firm promise to pay it back within a fixed time. He is inclined to make such a promise; but he has still enough conscience to ask "Is it not unlawful and contrary to duty to get out of difficulties in this way?" Supposing, however, he did resolve to do so, the maxim of his action would run thus, "Whenever I believe myself short of money, I will borrow money and promise to pay it back, though I know that this will never be done." Now this principle of self-love or personal advantage is perhaps quite compatible with my own entire future welfare; only there remains the question "Is it right?" I therefore transform the demand of self-love into a universal law and frame my question thus, "How would things stand if my maxim became a universal law?" I then see straight away that this maxim can never rank as a universal law of nature and be self-consistent, but must necessarily contradict itself. For the universality of a law that every one believing himself to be in need can make any promise he

pleases with the intention not to keep it would make promising, and the very purpose of promising, itself impossible, since no one would believe he was being promised anything, but would laugh at utterances of this kind as empty shams.[5]

It is important to be clear exactly what Kant is saying in this passage. He is not objecting to insincere promises on the ground that they will cause others to lose confidence in us and mean that we will jeopardize the valuable consequences of future promises. This would be to argue as an act utilitarian. Nor is he arguing that false promises contribute to a general mistrust of promises and the eventual collapse of a valuable social practice and the general rules upon which it is based. This would be to argue as a rule utilitarian. Such **consequentialist** arguments are, according to the deontologist Kant, totally irrelevant to questions of moral obligation.

Kant's point is a very different one. He is suggesting that a state of affairs in which everyone in need makes false promises is logically impossible or incoherent. There is a **contradiction** in this state of affairs because, on the one hand, everyone in need **would** borrow on false promises. They would be following the maxim "as a law of nature," with the same regularity as the planets observe the laws of planetary motion. Yet on the other hand, in this very same state of affairs no one **could** borrow on a false promise, because if such promises were always insincere, no one would be stupid enough to lend any money. Promising requires trust on the part of the one to whom the promise is made, but in the state of affairs contemplated there just could not be any, and so promises of the sort in question would simply be impossible. Hence any attempt to will, as a universal law of nature, the maxim "Whenever I believe myself short of money, I will borrow money and promise to pay it back, though I know that this will never be done," lands us in a logical contradiction. "I ... see straight away that this maxim can never rank as a universal law of nature and be self-consistent, but must necessarily contradict itself."[6]

Kant's Categorical Imperative provides us with a moral test of our actions which does not lie in an assessment of their consequences, in their utility. Nor does the test lie in weighing the consequences of adopting a general rule which licences those actions. Rather the test considers the logical coherence of the universalized maxim upon which I personally propose to act.[7] Whether this test successfully accounts for all of our moral obligations is perhaps questionable. Off hand, there seems nothing inconsistent in the state of affairs in which everyone assaults his neighbour if she persists in playing her stereo at ear-piercing levels. Such a state of affairs might be highly **undesirable** (though some days I really do wonder) but it seems perfectly **possible** or **conceivable**. It is unlike the state of affairs in which everyone **does** issue false promises if in need while no one **can** do so. Yet assaulting annoying neighbours seems hardly the right thing to do.

The Golden Rule

Despite the difficulties inherent in Kant's first formulation of the Categorical Imperative test, it does bring to light an important requirement of valid moral judgments which is endorsed by most moral theorists. The appropriate test of valid moral judgments, and the moral conduct they require or endorse, may not be whether my universalized maxim leads to logical contradiction. But most people, including most moral philosophers, will agree with the following implication of Kant's test: that I cannot morally act on a reason (a maxim) unless I am prepared to accept that everyone else in exactly my situation should act on that reason too. If I am not willing to agree that **everyone** should do what I propose to do in the circumstances in which I find myself, then I am bound by logical consistency to reject the claim that **I** may do so.

As we noted in Chapter 2, the non-cognitivist philosopher R.M. Hare seized upon this important feature of moral judgments—their universalizability—to fashion a powerful ethical theory which would have us test our moral judgments by seeing if we can assent to the implications of our universalized moral judgments. We are, Hare says, to see if we can live with the implications of the universalized prescriptions or principles upon which we propose to act. As Hare points out, among the most important implications of my consistently acting on a universal moral principle is my willingness to have other people act upon it **when it is I who am on the receiving end**. I must, for example, be willing to assent to the possibility that one of **my** friend's will lie to me in order to prevent **my** distress. If my reaction to such a possibility is to declare: "No way, I always want to be told the truth, even if the truth hurts!" then I cannot accept, as my reason for telling a lie to my friend, that I will spare him great distress. The theories of Kant and Hare bring to light, and explain the insight behind, a widely endorsed rule of moral thinking usually referred to as **The Golden Rule**. According to this rule, "one should do unto others only that which one is prepared to have them do unto you." Both Kant's first formulation of his Categorical Imperative, and Hare's requirement that we be willing to live with the implications of our universalized judgments, provide theoretical underpinning to this popular moral rule.[8]

The Categorical Imperative II: Respect for Persons

Kant provided two further formulations of his Categorical Imperative. He thought these versions equivalent to the first, though it is difficult to see why Kant thought this to be so. The equivalence question need not concern us here however. The additional formulations bring to light two important principles which figure in many ethical theories and moral codes.

According to Kant, if I act only on maxims which could, without contradiction, serve as universal laws, I will never treat people as **mere means** to my ends or objectives. The Categorical Imperative requires that I "[a]ct in such a way that [I] always treat humanity, whether in [my] own person or in the person of any other, never simply as a means, but always at the same time as an end."[9] In more common terms, we should never just **use** people. Rather, we should respect them as **persons**. The emphasis here is on the **intrinsic worth** and **dignity** of rational creatures. I treat rational beings as ends in themselves if I respect in them the same value I discover in myself, namely, my freedom to determine myself to action, that is, to act for reasons which I judge for myself. Sometimes this ability to exercise and act upon reasons for action is described as our **autonomy**. As autonomous creatures we are able to behave as "self-legislators." We are able to subject ourselves, not to the will of others, but to the requirements of right reason which we can discover for ourselves using our own intellect. As Kant observes, there can be nothing more dreadful to a rational creature than that his actions should be subject to the will of another. I treat others as mere things rather than as persons, subject them to my will in the way I do a tool, whenever I fail to respect their dignity.[10]

Here's an example which serves to illustrate Kant's powerful point. Suppose I am a physician who is taking part in a clinical trial testing the effectiveness of a new drug. I am having difficulty getting people to sign on to the trial. It then occurs to me that my practice of revealing all the possible side effects of the new drug is actually scaring my patients away. Although I tell them that the worst side effects are all extremely rare, my patients are ignoring these low probabilities and focusing instead on the effects themselves. I conclude that their reasoning is faulty, they are being misled by the vividness of the possible (though highly unlikely) side effects. As a result, I decide to gloss over that part of my presentation which deals with these immensely unlikely side effects. I attempt to justify this in the following way: if my patients were thinking rationally, they would all agree that the chance of the highly undesirable side effects taking place is in each instance very slight and well worth taking for the sake of the likely benefits. These are benefits which are likely to extend not only to my patients but to all those who will benefit later once the drug has been approved for general use. According to Kant, it is **my** reasoning that is faulty. In acting on my proposed maxim I would be using my patients as mere means to my own ends, and in so doing would have denied their intrinsic worth and dignity as rational agents. I would have, in effect, acted **paternalistically** towards them, thus violating the second formulation of the Categorical Imperative.

Categorical Imperative III

Kant's third formulation of the Categorical Imperative is closely tied to the second. In effect, it spells out what it is in rational agents which gives them their dignity and worth. It requires that we treat others as **autonomous** agents, capable of self-directed, rational action. The capacity to rise above the compelling forces of desire, self-interest, and physical necessity—to act freely on the basis of **reasons**—is what gives rational beings their dignity and worth. To treat a person as an end in herself, then, is to respect her autonomy and freedom. As noted, it rules out various kinds of manipulative practices and paternalistically motivated behaviours. Consider a case involving asbestos poisoning at Johns Manville.[11] Company doctors neglected to tell workers the alarming results of their medical tests. This was rationalized on the ground that there was nothing that could be done to curb the disease anyway, and so the workers were better off not knowing. Such paternalistic conduct clearly violated the third (and second) formulation(s) of Kant's Categorical Imperative. It failed to respect the autonomy and dignity of the asbestos workers. Of course the conduct might have been fully justified by AU and possibly RU, though this point is open to argument. Whether in the long run such deceptions serve to maximize utility is perhaps questionable.

Summing Up

With Kant we have a clear alternative to the monistic, teleological theory of obligation provided by the act and rule utilitarians. Kant's theory is clearly deontological and is at the very least monistic in its intent. Kant attempts to ground all our obligations on one fundamental principle: the Categorical Imperative. As we have seen, Kant provides three formulations of this principle, though it is not easy to see how they are exactly equivalent. In any event, we may view Kant as requiring that a moral agent always ask the following three questions when attempting to determine what she ought to do:

1. Could I consistently will, as a universal law, the personal maxim upon which I propose to act?

2. Would my action degrade other rational agents or myself by treating them (or myself) as a mere means?

3. Would my action violate the autonomy of some rational agent, possibly myself?

Should any of these three questions yield the wrong answer, my moral obligation is to refrain from acting on my personal maxim.

A Brief Assessment

There is much in Kant's moral theory that is insightful, even if there is also much that is controversial and obscure. The fundamental insight of Categorical Imperative I, that we must not act on maxims which we are not prepared to have others act on as well, highlights at least two fundamental requirements of valid moral thinking accepted by most moral agents. It captures not only the requirement of logical consistency, but also the requirement of **impartiality** which is accepted by many as an integral aspect of the moral life. Unlike the dictates of prudence, which allow for a kind of partiality towards my own interests and the interests of those about whom I care, Categorical Imperative I requires me to be impartial with respect to all rational creatures. In particular, it prevents me from ever making **exceptions** for myself or for those I care about. If I am not prepared to see everyone in circumstances like mine share in the advantages I seek—act on the maxim upon which I propose to act—then morality prohibits me from doing so. In highlighting this important insight, Kant has done us a great service.

Categorical Imperatives II and III both highlight what is, for many people, a further important feature of moral life: the intrinsic worth or value of human beings. Kant has been criticized for locating the locus of this value exclusively in our **rationality**, and ignoring other aspects of nature and life, both human and non-human. If it is rationality which provides an agent with moral dignity or worth, then it seems we must omit from the realm of our moral considerations animals and human beings whose rationality is absent or limited. But most enlightened individuals are loathe to accept this implication, thus challenging Kant's identification of our moral worth with our capacity to exercise reason.[12] Despite this shortcoming of Kant's theory, he should no doubt be applauded for stressing the idea that the worth and dignity of human beings does not lie in their capacity to experience pleasure or happiness alone. Perhaps he should also be applauded for encouraging us to think hard about whether there is more to moral judgment than an assessment of consequences. Sometimes the very nature of a proposed course of action, as expressed in its maxim, determines its moral status. Contemporary deontological theories typically follow Kant's lead in asserting that more than consequences count. They depart from him, however, in their willingness to say that consequences do count sometimes and to some extent, even if not always and exclusively. One such theory is the mixed deontological theory of W.D. Ross to which we now turn.

Notes

1. See Hume's *A Treatise of Human Nature*, ed. L.A. Selby-Biggs (Oxford: Oxford University Press, 1973). See in particular, Book III,

Seven :: *The Deontological Ethics of Immanuel Kant*

Section II of the *Treatise*, "Moral Distinctions deriv'd from a moral sense." Book III was originally published in 1740, Books I and II in 1739.

2. Immanuel Kant, *Groundwork of the Metaphysics of Morals*, trans. H.J. Paton (New York: Harper and Row, 1964), 67-68.

3. *Ibid.*, 70.

4. *Ibid.*, 89.

5. *Ibid.*, 89-90.

6. *Ibid.*, 90. Kant says that the maxim involved in false promising is itself contradictory. But in other cases he suggests, not that the maxim is contradictory, but that the agent's **will** is in some way contradictory or inconsistent. It isn't that the agent wills a universalized maxim, A, which is inconsistent. Rather, there is a conflict between the act of willing A and the act of willing something else, B. For example, if I attempt to will, as universal law, a maxim which permits individuals to ignore those in distress, my act of will will be inconsistent with something else which I (perhaps necessarily) will: that someone should help **me** if I ever should find myself in distress. Such an alternative account places Kant more squarely in line with other contemporary philosophers like R.M. Hare, who stress the universalizability of moral judgments and reasons (see pp. 176-77). For detailed accounts of Kant's views on the contradictions involved in willing immoral maxims, see H.J. Paton, *The Categorical Imperative* (London: Hutchinson & Co., 1947); O. O'Neill, *Constructions of Reason: Explorations of Kant's Practical Philosophy* (Cambridge: Cambridge University Press, 1989); and C. Korsgaard, *Creating the Kingdom of Ends* (Cambridge: Cambridge University Press, 1996).

7. Or the logical consistency between what I purport universally to will and something else which I (perhaps necessarily) will.

8. Henry Sidgwick provides an insightful account of what he regards as the self-evident element of the golden rule. See H. Sidgwick, *The Methods of Ethics*, 7th ed. (London: Macmillan, 1906), pp. 379-80.

9. *Groundwork*, 96.

10. It might be asked whether Kant's focus on **rational** creatures adequately captures our commitment to the intrinsic worth of those who have yet to achieve rationality (e.g., small infants) or those who may never do so (e.g., animals and those who suffer severe cognitive impairment). It might also be questioned whether his focus on rationality leaves out the more emotional, caring side of moral life. These are points to which we will return in Chapter 10 below.

11. See Lloyd Tataryn, "From Dust to Dust," in D. Poff and W. Waluchow, eds., *Business Ethics in Canada* (Scarborough: Prentice-Hall, 1987), 122-25.

12. Similar complaints have been made against social contract theories. If the demands of morality arise from a contract among **rational**, self-interested individuals, then where does this leave all those beings who are not rational? And what does it say about the non-rational aspects of human personality and relations?

Eight
The Ethical Pluralism of W.D. Ross

Ross's Fundamental Insight:
The Complexity of Moral Life

Moral life is complex. It is not an easy matter to determine our moral obligations, duties and rights, or to decide which virtues are worthy of pursuit and cultivation or which ideals are worthy of emulation. If we could somehow reduce all moral issues to one fundamental question, as the utilitarians, Kantians, and the Divine Command theorists suggest, then our quest for a successful moral life would be far easier than it appears to be. In discerning the requirements of morality we could ask just one question: "Does this act maximize utility?" "Does this act conform with a rule whose general observance would maximize utility?" "Can the maxim of my action be universalized without contradiction?" or "Does this action comply with the commands of God?" Discerning our moral responsibilities would still be difficult in many cases, but at least we would know which question to ask and how to go about answering it.

But as we have repeatedly seen throughout this book, moral life is not quite that simple. Do consequences matter in the moral assessment of our conduct? Of course, they do. It matters that telling a lie to a friend may prevent terrible consequences. If I tell my suicidal friend where his gun is hidden, he will likely kill himself in an act of desperation. Surely these consequences matter and so any theory, such as Kant's which excludes such considerations entirely, seems clearly inadequate or incomplete. But does this mean, in the end, that consequences are the **only** things that matter as Mill and Bentham would have it? Again, the answer seems to be clear. Of course not. Sometimes, for example, the intentions with which we act seem to matter. It matters that the President's choice to shoot down a domestic airliner to prevent hijackers from plunging it into an office tower amounts to the intentional killing of many innocent people. The same can be said of the special relationships we share with others such as our families, friends, patients and clients. These seem to matter in ways which may not, in the end, adequately be cashed out in terms of consequences. Justice also seems to matter. It just seems wrong to frame an innocent man for a heinous crime, even if the result of not doing so is the loss of numerous lives.

Ross's moral theory arose mainly from his awareness of the multiple factors which seem to play a role in our moral thinking. In particular, it arose from a dissatisfaction with attempts to reduce morality to the single question posed by the utilitarians: Does this action (or rule) maximize utility? While Ross's main target was G.E. Moore, his criticisms are relevant to utilitarianism (and, by extension, consequentialism) in general. According to Ross, utilitarianism in all of its guises grossly oversimplifies the moral relationships among people. Utilitarianism errs in thinking that "the only morally significant relationship in which my neighbours stand to me is that of being possible beneficiaries [or victims] of my action."[1] It errs, in other words, in being a monistic, teleological theory of obligation. Ross proposes instead a pluralistic theory of obligation which recognizes several irreducible moral relationships, duties and principles. Nothing less than this multiplicity can do justice to the complexities of moral life. In addition to their role as possible beneficiaries of my actions, my fellow human beings "may also stand to me in the relation of promisee to promiser, of creditor to debtor, of wife to husband, of child to parent, of friend to friend, of fellow countryman to fellow countryman, and the like."[2] "The like" no doubt includes the relation of doctor to patient, lawyer to client, experimenter to subject, Member of Parliament to constituent, teacher to student, and so on. All these relationships are integral aspects of the moral life.

In Ross's view, utilitarianism not only oversimplifies the moral relationships in which we stand to others, it also distorts the whole basis of morality by being thoroughly teleological in orientation. Recall that on utilitarian theories we must, in the final analysis, always be **forward-looking** to the future consequences of our actions or rules. But sometimes, Ross urges, morality requires that we look **backwards** to what has occurred in the past. There is significance, for example, in the sheer fact that a promise has been made, a promise which has a moral force independent of any future good consequences that might arise from keeping it. This moral force explains why we should normally keep promises made to dying friends even if utility would be maximized were we to break them. A promise itself, because of the **kind** of action that it is, has a moral significance independent of its consequences. Teleological or consequentialist theories, because they ignore such features and are entirely forward-looking, distort morality. **Promises, contracts, commitments** to serve a certain role, **agreements, loyalty, friendship** and so on all have moral significance, and all can give rise to obligations and responsibilities independently of good or bad consequences.

Ross's Solution: Mixed Deontological Theory

Ross provides us, then, with a pluralistic, mixed deontological theory of obligation. In this theory we find a plurality of ultimate principles, only some of which are consequentialist in orientation. According to Ross, each of these principles specifies what he calls a **prima facie** duty or obligation. These are duties which we must fulfil **unless** we are also, in the circumstances, subject to another, competing prima facie duty of greater weight. We have a prima facie duty to tell the truth, which means that we must always tell the truth **unless** a more stringent duty applies to us and requires a falsehood. An example from Kant helps to illustrate this feature nicely.

Kant is notorious for arguing that the Categorical Imperative establishes an unconditional duty always to tell the truth. He has us consider a case where a murderer comes to our door asking for the whereabouts of his intended victim. Should we tell him the truth—that the victim is seeking refuge in our house—and thereby become accomplices in his murder? Both AU and RU would undoubtedly licence a lie under such extraordinary circumstances, but according to Kant the Categorical Imperative does not. The duty to tell the truth is unconditional, despite the consequences of its observance. "To be truthful (honest) in all declarations ... is a sacred and absolutely commanding decree of reason, limited by no expediency."[3] According to Ross this just cannot be right. Kant's case is clearly one where our prima facie duty to be truthful is overridden or outweighed by more stringent duties to our friend. These include, presumably, principles governing friendship and the avoidance of great harm to other people.

Ross's list of prima facie duties provides a helpful classification of some of the various duties and morally significant relationships recognized in our everyday moral thinking.[4] There are, he says:

1. Duties resting on previous actions of our own. These include:

    (a) duties of **fidelity** arising from explicit or implicit promises;

    (b) duties of **reparation**, resting on previous wrongful acts of ours and requiring that we compensate, as best we can, the victims of our wrongful conduct.

2. Duties resting on the services of others: duties of **gratitude** which require that we return favour for favour.

3. Duties involving the **fair** distribution of goods: duties of **justice**, which require fair sharing of goods to be distributed.

4. Duties to improve the condition of others: duties of **beneficence** (which in part form the basis of utilitarian theories of obligation).

5. Duties to improve our own condition: duties of **self-improvement**.

6. Duties not to injure others; duties of **non-malefi-cence**.[5]

Ross's list of duties is less than exhaustive, and no doubt many would quarrel with some of its content. For instance, it might be questioned whether duties of self-improvement belong on a list of **moral** duties. It is plausible to suppose that moral duties arise only in our relationships with other people—that the demands of morality govern **inter-personal** relationships only. Allowing one's talents to lie unused or allowing one's health to deteriorate may be imprudent or foolish, but is it immoral? Perhaps it is if others, say our children, are depending on us. But in this case it is not a moral duty of self-improvement which is violated but rather duties such as the duties of beneficence and possibly non-maleficence, or special duties we have to family members and those who are dependent on us. Another questionable candidate is the duty to be grateful. If someone does me a favour, is it true that I am required, as a matter of duty, to be grateful? One might question whether gratitude is something that can be subject to duty. Perhaps instead it is something that must be freely given, given not out of a sense of duty but out of genuine, heartfelt goodwill. If a favour is done with the sense that something is **owing** as a result, then perhaps it is not really a favour at all, but an investment.

In any case, the intention here is not to take issue with Ross's list, only to suggest that specific items are perhaps open to question. This leads to a point of some significance. According to Ross, that we have the prima facie duties he mentions is simply **self-evident** to any rational human being who thinks seriously about the requirements of morality. The existence of these duties and the validity of the principles which describe them are known through **moral intuition**.

Eight :: *The Ethical Pluralism of W.D. Ross*

To say that a principle is self-evident and known through intuition is to say that its truth is evident to an attentive mind, that it neither needs supporting evidence nor needs to be deduced from other propositions. It stands alone as something obviously true. In this instance it stands alone as something whose truth is known directly through **moral** intuition. It will be recalled that Aquinas held that the primary principles of the natural law, e.g., that human beings ought to live together in society, are in this way self-evident.

This feature of Ross's theory is very controversial among philosophers, who are generally suspicious of "self-evident principles" and "intuition." To some, the apparent obviousness of the principles underlying Ross's duties and the certainty with which many believe them seem better explained by such things as uniform moral upbringing and common experiences. Moral conventionalists will go so far as to assert that Ross's principles only appear self-evident to him because of the culture in which he was raised. This was a culture in which the duties he mentions were widely accepted and practiced, and were therefore "valid" for that culture or society—assuming, of course, that his list accurately reflects uniform moral beliefs and practices. But, of course, one need not be a moral conventionalist to be suspicious of Ross's claim that his principles are self-evident. If a principle truly is self-evident, then should not everyone agree on its validity? Yet this is seldom, if ever, the case with moral principles, including those underlying Ross's list.

This is not the place to discuss further the reasons behind philosophers' suspicions concerning self-evidence and moral intuition, except to add the following. One who claims self-evidence for his views has little to say to those holding conflicting "self-evident" claims. She can ask that we think again, but she cannot undertake to prove her claims to us.

If her claims truly are self-evident and known through intuition, they are in need of no proof. Perhaps more importantly, none can be given. So if, after careful reflection, you continue to disagree with some of the duties on Ross's list, he has little recourse but to accuse you of moral blindness. He must view you as equivalent to a person who cannot see the difference between red and green; your moral blindness is on a par with his colour blindness. One might ask whether this is a satisfactory response to serious moral disagreements among reasonable people of good will and integrity. Would we not be better served by a theory, such as utilitarianism or social contract theory, each of which would provide us with some way of addressing inevitable cases of disagreement? Take, for instance, a social contract theory of the kind espoused by Hobbes and Gauthier. This theory has, at least in principle, a way of solving disagreements over the validity of moral principles, including those underlying the duties on Ross's list. We are to ask, in each case in which there is disagreement: Is this a principle with which a group of rational individuals would agree as a satisfactory means of removing themselves from prisoner's dilemma type situations? Better this question than a resort to accusations of moral blindness. On the other hand, a defender of Ross might ask: How valuable is this method when disagreement will inevitably reappear over the question whether social contract theory provides us with the **correct** way of resolving moral disagreements? Are we really any better off with the contract theorist's so-called solution?

A Question of Balance:
Weighing Prima Facie Duties

Ross believed that his self-evident principles articulate prima facie moral obligations. These are obligations which hold unless overridden in individual cases by a more stringent or weightier duty. As for how we are to determine which of two or more prima facie duties has greater weight in a given case, Ross provides no answer except to say that we must use our best judgment. This is of little help because it fails to tell us the considerations upon which our judgments should be based. Ross is fully aware that in most cases of conflicting obligations it is far from clear which duty is more stringent. Reasonable people of moral integrity will disagree. We therefore seem left with a serious gap in the theory, and must either accept that in cases of conflict there is no one right thing to do — that the best we can do is fulfil one of our conflicting duties and violate the other — or we must continue to look for a **criterion** in terms of which conflicts can be resolved. Presumably the first option is to be avoided if at all possible. There may be times when we are indeed faced with moral dilemmas — where whatever we do we seem to do something wrong, where we are "damned if we do, and damned if we don't." But surely such cases are very much the exception not the rule, as they would be were we to accept the first option. So we should, unless forced to do otherwise, opt for the second option. We should look for a criterion in terms of which competing principles can be weighed against each other. Among the principal aims of a moral theory is to tell us how, in principle at least, we should go about determining our moral obligations. A theory which simply tells us that there is often no right answer to the question "What should I do?" only a series of different answers each of which involves violation of a moral obligation, seems clearly inadequate.

It is at this point that the utilitarian and the social contract theorist will be more than happy to offer assistance. Take the utilitarian. In her view, Ross has compiled for us a plausible set of duties and corresponding principles which are indeed important in everyday moral thinking. According to the defender of AU, these Rossian principles are useful **guidelines** or **rules of thumb** which we are well advised in most cases to follow. Indeed, we do well, according to most defenders of AU, to inculcate in ourselves and those for whose moral education we are responsible, the habit or tendency to rely on these principles in all but highly unusual cases.[6] There are two principal reasons why this is so. First, it is not always possible to know, with any degree of certainty, what the specific consequences of an act will in fact be, making a utilitarian calculation difficult. Rules of thumb provide an indication of what courses of action **generally** advance utility; and so if we follow them we are more likely to do the right thing. Second, human nature being what it is, we are apt in many instances to make exceptions to moral rules and principles when doing so will serve our own interests or the interests of those we care about. It is therefore a good strategy, for ensuring that we more often than not do the right thing, to **condition ourselves** to obey Ross's rules of thumb in all but the most exceptional of cases. If we follow this strategy faithfully, then our actions will in the long run end up maximizing utility. The act of keeping a promise almost always does maximize utility, as does a display of gratitude. And this is no less true in those many cases where breaking the promise or deciding not to show gratitude will work against our own self-interest. As for those exceptional cases in which a genuine conflict in our generally acceptable principles does arise, or where following an applicable principle seems clearly inappropriate for good utilitarian reasons, we must resort directly to the AU criterion and decide which action will maximize utility.[7]

Consider now the proponent of RU. She will likely claim that (at least most of) Ross's principles will almost certainly figure in a set of rules (or principles) general observance of which within a modern society will maximize utility. Like her AU counterpart, she is likely to claim that, in cases in which the rules conflict, direct recourse must be made to the principle of utility. And if, as is all too common, the rules stand in need of interpretation because a new application question has arisen, then, once again, appeal must be made to the master principle — the principle of utility.[8] After all, it is the basis upon which the rules are themselves justified, so it makes eminently good sense to appeal to that principle in hard cases where the rules offer inadequate guidance. Finally, the social contract theorist will offer, as a solution to Ross's quandry, the strategy posed in Chapter 5. He will suggest that we ask the following question: Which resolution of the relevant conflict of principles would be agreed upon, in advance, by a group of rational contractors concerned to extricate themselves from the state of nature?

Ross must reject all these lines of defence against the charge of incompleteness. Were he to follow the utilitarian's lead he would in effect be adopting the principle of utility as defining a single, ultimate obligation, and this would be to deny Ross's central claim that each of his prima facie duties is ultimate and irreducible. Similar things would be said in response to the social contract theorist's offer of assistance. But then it is far from clear how this plurality of irreducible duties is to be dealt with in cases of conflict. We seem left with a serious gap. Without a means of adjudicating among conflicting prima facie duties, we are left short just where we need guidance the most.

Notes

1. W.D. Ross, *The Right and the Good* (Oxford: Oxford University Press, 1930), 21.

2. *Ibid.*, 13.

3. Immanuel Kant, "On a Supposed Right to Lie from Altruistic Motives," in L.W. Beck, ed., *Critique of Practical Reason and Other Writings in Moral Philosophy* (Chicago: University of Chicago Press, 1949), 346-50.

4. Many utilitarians (and consequentialists generally) will find Ross's list perfectly acceptable, either as useful rules of thumb (AU; direct consequentialism) or principles the general observance of which yields maximum utility (RU; indirect consequentialism). More on this below.

5. *The Right and the Good*, 21.

6. For more on this, see the preceding chapter.

7. For a highly developed theory along these lines, see, once again, R.M. Hare's *Moral Thinking*.

8. For a discussion of "application questions" see Chapter 3 above where we explored, in the context of analysing the merits of moral relativism, some of the central features of moral thinking. An example of an application question is the question of whether removing life support from a person in a persistent vegetative state would amount to harm and therefore violate the principle of non-maleficence (6 on Ross's list).

Nine
The Virtue Ethics of Aristotle

"What Should I Be" not "What Should I Do"

Despite their many differences, the theories of Kant, Ross and the utilitarians had at least one thing in common: they were all designed to answer directly the question "What should I do?" In other words, each philosopher was concerned, in the main, with providing a viable theory of obligation, the aim of which was to help us determine which actions we should perform in any situation in which we find ourselves. According to Kant the question "What should I do?" is answered by determining whether the maxim of one's action can be universalized. For rule utilitarians the answer lies in whether the rule under which one acts figures in a set of rules the adoption of which will maximize overall utility. Although act utilitarians believe that rules have no role in our moral reasoning, except as rules of thumb, the question remains: "What is the right thing for me to do in these circumstances?" According to act utilitarians, we answer this question by determining which of the actions open to us would maximize utility. Ross too was concerned to help us determine what we should do in particular circumstances, that is, the course of (right) action wherein our moral duty lies. Modern theories sometimes transform the questions of Mill, Ross, and Kant into questions about our rights, but still the emphasis is on the evaluation of **actions**, and the **rules** and **principles** which tell us which actions to perform.

Much earlier in the history of moral philosophy the Greek philosopher Aristotle sought to cast ethics in an entirely different mould. This is a mould which some contemporary moral philosophers find highly appealing, partly because it allows us to avoid many of the difficulties encountered by the traditional deontological and utilitarian theories, but also because it is thought to provide a much better understanding of our moral lives: what it is we strive to be in pursuing the moral life and why the moral life is important to us. The fundamental ethical question for Aristotle was not "What should I **do**?" but "What should I **be**?" As one similarly minded theorist put it:

> ... morality is internal. The moral law ... has to be expressed in the form, "be this," not in the form "do this." ... [T]he true moral law says "hate not," instead of "kill not." ... [T]he only mode of stating the moral law must be as a rule of character.[1]

For Aristotle, moral behaviour expresses **virtues** or qualities of **character**. There is a much greater emphasis on "character traits" and "types of persons," than on rules, obligations, duties, and rights. Aristotle is interested in questions such as these: Should we **be** selfish or generous? Hateful or benevolent? Cowardly or courageous? Over-indulgent or temperate? In what do these traits consist? How are they cultivated? And how do they figure in a life well lived? In discussing these questions about the character traits integral to a life well lived, Aristotle offered exemplars of virtue to emulate and vices to avoid rather than rules or principles to be obeyed or disobeyed. In short, for Aristotle, morality is **character oriented** rather than **rule driven**. Aristotle would no doubt have frowned on modern ethical theories which divorce actions and questions about them from the character of the agents who perform them. Praiseworthy and blameworthy actions are not those which match up to a particular template of rules or principles. Rather, they are ones which flow from, and reveal, a certain type of character. Moral agency is not merely a matter of which rules or principles to follow; it flows from a whole way of life which requires a unity of thought and feeling characteristic of what Aristotle called the virtuous life.

Theoretical and Practical Reason

Aristotle was no skeptic when it came to morality. Just as we can know certain truths about the nature of the universe — say about the stars and planets above us — or about the eternal truths of mathematics, we can know certain moral truths. Just as his devotee, St. Thomas Aquinas, later held, it is possible, Aristotle thought, to have knowledge of virtue. This is not to say, however, that Aristotle did not see any difference at all between our knowledge of mathematical or logical truths and our knowledge of virtue. In fact, he divided knowledge into two different kinds: the theoretical and the practical. Theoretical knowledge, or **episteme**, is concerned with speculative or theoretical inquiries, and its object is knowledge of the truth (about planets, numbers, and so on). This he contrasted with **phronesis** or practical knowledge which focuses on what is **doable** rather than on what is **knowable** for its own sake. Without **phronesis**, particular virtues of character (e.g., courage, moderation and generosity) would not be achievable by human beings, and the conduct which flows from and expresses these virtues would not be likely. It is central to Aristotle's view of human knowledge and moral excellence that whereas the intellectual virtues associated with **episteme** can be acquired exclusively through teaching, the virtues of character achievable via phronesis require practice until they become "second nature." Moral virtue can not just be taught as one can teach the basic principles of logic or physics; it requires "training" and "habituation," the doing of virtuous actions. In order to be a virtuous person one must develop the disposition to be virtuous.[2]

Human Good

Aristotle's ethical theory is clearly teleological. "Every art and every inquiry, every action and choice, seems to aim at some good; whence the good has rightly been defined as that at which all things aim."[3] There are different goods corresponding to the various arts and modes of inquiry. Navigation aims at safe voyages, the musical arts at the creation of beautiful music, and the medical arts aim at health. Is there, Aristotle asks, a good for human beings as such? If so, then perhaps we can begin to understand what we might call "the art of living well" by considering what is necessary to the achievement of that end. Just as we can understand proper medical practice in relation to the good which medicine strives to achieve, perhaps we can also understand moral life in relation to the good for human persons which moral life strives to achieve. So Aristotle is interested in action in so far as it contributes to the good for human beings. The right thing to do is best understood in relation to what is conducive to the good for human beings, just as a "proper prescription" is best understood in relation to what is conducive to a patient's health.

In his classic work, the *Nicomachean Ethics,* Aristotle confines his discussion of the good—that at which all things aim—to human good.[4] The good aimed at by human beings is **eudaemonia**, usually translated as "happiness" or "well-being."[5] Some people identify human good with such things as wealth, pleasure and honour, but Aristotle quickly shows that these people cannot be right. Wealth, for example, is at best a (very unreliable) means to happiness, not happiness itself, as many instant lottery winners soon learn. Pleasure is also not the good for human beings even though it is true, as Aristotle's teacher Plato argued, that the good person normally takes pleasure in virtuous activity. Recall a similar point which emerged earlier in Chapter 2 above when we discussed the validity of hedonism as a theory of value. Marcie takes pleasure in her children because she values them and the relationships she shares with them. She does not value her children because of the pleasure they sometimes bring her. For Aristotle, then, pleasure is not itself the good, but only an external sign of the presence of goodness. One will (typically) experience pleasure when one does things well; but doing well does not consist in the achievement of pleasure.

Yet another feature of Aristotle's account of eudaemonia is that it is not a transient state, like the happiness I experience in watching the latest movie blockbuster with my friends. In his sense of the term, happiness or well-being is something enjoyed over a lifetime in the exercise of virtues such as courage, moderation and generosity of spirit. In one sense it is true that the exercise of the virtues is a means to the achievement of happiness or well-being. Yet in a much deeper sense it is not. The exercise of virtue is integral to the achievement of happiness, **constitutive** of it, not merely a pre-payment of dues to insure later happiness as on some versions of consequentialism. In short, the virtuous life is not, for Aristotle, a means to the end of well-being; it **is** the life of well-being. Virtue, as many say, is its own reward.

Virtue

Central to the Aristotelian conception of ethics and the good life is, as we have seen, the notion of "virtue." Aristotle's definition of this key notion is as follows. Virtue is "a state of character concerned with choice, lying in a mean, i.e., the mean relative to us, this being determined by a rational principle, that principle by which the [person] of practical wisdom would determine it ..."[6] The key notions in this definition need to be clarified.

A fundamental element in Aristotle's conception of virtue is "disposition." Virtue is a kind of disposition. William Frankena nicely summarizes the nature of dispositions as follows:

> ... dispositions or traits ... are not wholly innate; they
> must all be acquired, at least in part, by teaching and
> practice, or perhaps by grace. They are also traits of
> "character," rather than traits of "personality" like
> charm or shyness, and they all involve a tendency to
> do certain kinds of action in certain kinds of situations,
> not just to think or feel in certain ways. They are not
> just abilities or skills, like intelligence or carpentry,
> which one may have without using.[7]

Linguistically, terms describing dispositions are often contrasted with "occurrence" terms. Applying a dispositional term like "timid" to a person says a good deal more about him than the application of the occurrence word "frightened." The former tells us something about the character of the individual whereas the latter may tell us nothing more than that the person was in a particular state on some occasion or other. It is possible that the state we might call "Ted's being frightened" occurred on some occasion even though Ted has no disposition to be frightened. Very little future behaviour can be predicted from being told that someone is frightened or angry, even if we know the reasons why he is frightened or angry. On the other hand, if we are told that Becky is timid or irascible, then we can predict that she will tend to get frightened or angry in circumstances that would not frighten or anger other people with more courageous or gentler dispositions. Having such dispositions does not, of course, rule out the possibility of sometimes acting "out of character." There are provocations that would try even the patience of Job, some tasks so dangerous as to deter the most courageous and resolute persons, and some offers that even the most conscientious person cannot refuse. Dispositions, as tendencies, have a degree of elasticity about them.

Aristotle's definition of virtue begins with virtue as a disposition, but it does not end there. Virtue is a disposition **to choose well**. Commenting on the etymology of the Greek word for choice, **proairesis**, Aristotle writes: "the very term **proairesis** ... denotes something chosen before other things."[8] Choosing something before other things requires (a) the presence of alternatives. Without alternatives there can be no choice. It also requires (b) deliberation about the relative merits of the alternatives open to the agent. Virtuous actions are principled and thoughtful, even if they are not **simply** acts which conform with valid principles. They are thoughtful responses rather than thoughtless reactions or mindless conformity with authoritative directives. Deliberation about the alternatives open to the agent requires (c) ranking those alternatives: one alternative is preferred to another and chosen on some basis which can be articulated via the expression of a moral judgment. Finally, **proairesis** presupposes (d) **voluntarism.** Virtue requires that we are responsible for our own actions. As Kant stressed, moral agents are the begetters or efficient causes of their own actions, agents not patients. In acting morally, our actions must be "self-caused," i.e., "in our power and voluntary."[9] In this respect, Aristotle's theory is very much like Kant's in stressing our autonomy as moral agents. Unlike Kant, however, it is thoroughly consequentialist or teleological in orientation.

Human Nature, Essentialism and Moral Relativism

Aristotle emphasizes that our practical choices are primarily restricted to means and not ends. The ultimate and remote end of all our choosing, **eudaemonia** or happiness, is fixed by human nature. Just as all things within the universe have an essential nature (understood by Aristotle in terms of a unique function the thing serves) in relation to which their "good" can be understood, human nature provides a natural basis for understanding the good for human beings.[10] This particular feature of Aristotle's view allows him to avoid moral relativism; morality is not based exclusively on variable social norms or customs, or on the personal predilections of individuals or groups of individuals. The fundamental elements of morality are not "culturally relative" or "subjective" according to Aristotle; they are grounded in nature and to that extent "objective." Variations in moral beliefs and practices do occur, but there are explanations of these variations which are consistent with a universal human nature and an account of the good based upon it. Explanations in terms of "corrupt habits," "evil persuasions," "faulty reasoning" and the various ways in which societies can "determine" general notions of the good are all as open to Aristotle as they were later to Aquinas.[11]

Although the "objectivity" of the Aristotelian schema allows Aristotle to avoid relativism, it is, as we noted earlier, a serious source of concern for some. Many critics see danger in the idea that there is a largely fixed, essential human nature in terms of which the moral life and the requirements it places upon us are to be understood. Some who claim an allegiance to Aristotle have argued that procreation is "natural" to human beings (as it is to all organisms) and that so-called "artificial" means of reproduction, such as in vitro fertilization, are therefore inherently suspicious and perhaps even immoral. Such an allegiance also motivates many who are now opposed to stem cell research on human embryos. That such activities threaten the "natural order" of human procreation and development is thought by some people to be a serious source of concern. A somewhat similar line of argument is sometimes taken in supporting the view that homosexuality is immoral. "Procreation is natural; natural procreation requires the involvement of a male and female; therefore, sexual activity among members of the same sex is unnatural and therefore morally wrong." Whether such views actually follow from the Aristotelian system, and whether Aristotle would himself accept the views attributed to his conception are highly questionable. But there is, nevertheless, cause to be concerned about a theory which seeks to define the moral in terms of what is "natural" for human beings. All too often what is thought to be "natural" for human beings is really only the conventional, or what is sanctioned by dominant groups or cultures. And as feminists and other social critics point out, these are often the result of bias, misunderstanding, and oppression.[12]

A Disguised Theory of Obligation?

If the ultimate end of our choosing is fixed by human nature, and the alternatives open to us when we seek to be virtuous are alternative ways of promoting this end, i.e., alternative ways of promoting **eudaemonia**, then the following question arises. Is Aristotle in actual fact advocating a consequentialist theory of obligation? Is he advocating what we might call the **principle of eudaemonia**, as opposed to the principle of utility? And is this not a principle which can be applied, either directly or indirectly, to our actions in such a way that we have a means of determining morally right actions? For example, particular virtues like truth-telling, promise-keeping, and their ilk could be viewed, as they would be by an indirect consequentialist like Hare, as a means of achieving the ultimate end of **eudaemonia** or happiness. If this is so, then in actual fact there may be little to distinguish Aristotle's so-called "virtue ethics" from the action-centred "duty ethics" of Mill and Hare.

Although there is some truth in this assessment of Aristotle's ethics, it would be a mistake to exaggerate it. And this is because, for Aristotle, virtuous action is not action which maps onto a principle whose adoption would maximize happiness. Rather it is action which springs from a disposition to choose a way which lies between two extremes, the one an excess and the other a deficiency. Virtuous action lies in choosing **the mean** between extremes of behaviour, one of which is a vice through excess, the other of which is a vice through deficiency. And Aristotle is clear that there is no arithmetical formula which allows us to determine with precision what lies at the mean in any particular set of circumstances. This is one reason why he says that the mean must be determined "relatively to us," and as determined not by a rule universally applicable and established in advance, but by a rule "by which a practically wise person would determine it." On Aristotle's account, there is a kind of **indeterminacy** in moral judgments when it comes to deciding on particular courses of action. The variable contexts of moral life prevent us from fashioning hard-and-fast rules or procedures for settling what we ought to do. The best we can do is rely on **phronesis**, our virtuous dispositions, and the examples set by moral paradigms. We must, in other words, try under the circumstances to act as "the person of practical reason would act." This is the best that we can do. Aristotle is, in effect, asking us to take on a role quite similar to that played by the human sovereign in Aquinas' natural law theory. Just as the sovereign must use her discretion to render more determinate what the natural law leaves open, we must, each of us and in our own way, render more determinate what it is to be virtuous in the various situations with which we are faced in the course of every-day living. And just as there may be no uniquely right answer for the sovereign to find, there may be no uniquely right answer for us to discover.

Indeterminacy—Deficiency or Strength?

Whether this inherent indeterminacy is a weakness in Aristotle's account of moral life is a difficult question to answer. As we saw earlier in relation to Ross's pluralistic theory of obligation, we do want our ethical theories to tell us what we should be doing with our lives. And we should, all else being equal, continue to search for right answers and a moral theory which provides them. But perhaps we should also acknowledge the possibility that morality and ethical theory have both practical and theoretical limits. If they do, then perhaps we are far better off acknowledging this fact, regrettable as it might be. It may well be that the indeterminacy inherent in Aristotle's account of the virtuous life better reflects moral reality and the perplexing dilemmas with which we are often faced than theories which purport to provide ready-made answers. Often the promised answers fail to emerge when we seek to apply the theories to concrete circumstances. Is it any more helpful to be told that one must maximize utility, or seek to treat humanity as an end in itself, than it is to be told that one must seek a mean between deficiency and excess? Think again of the President faced with the excruciating decision whether to bring down an airliner filled with innocent people in order to thwart the designs of the terrorists bent on crashing the plane into a crowded office tower. In explicitly acknowledging that morality can provide only limited assistance in answering such a question, that at the end of the day the President can perhaps do no more than aim for a mean point between deficiency and excess, seek guidance from the lives and decisions of individuals faced with similar decisions, and attempt to choose "as a practically wise person would choose," we may conclude that Aristotle's theory is in fact the more honest one.[13] We should seek precision only when it is available. And with moral life, it just may not always be available.

Virtue and the Doctrine of the Mean

Virtue lies at the mean point between the vices of excess and deficiency. The virtues are numerous and various and Aristotle does not attempt to provide a complete list of them. But such a list would undoubtedly include such traits of character as: **tolerance, courage, benevolence, friendliness, generosity, justice, loyalty, industriousness**, and **honesty**. Two virtues, courage and moderation (or temperance), are singled out by Aristotle to elucidate his doctrine of the mean. The accounts are perhaps dated, but they never-theless serve to illustrate the main lines of Aristotle's thought. Let's begin with courage.

For Aristotle, courage is primarily a virtue of soldiers and his examples are culled entirely from the battlefield. Courage is located between the defect of fear and the excess of over-spiritedness or brashness. When the occasion arises, a courageous soldier can be counted on to subdue fear and en-ter bravely into the fray even in the face of death. Cowardice is the vice (defect) associated with fear. In more modern par-lance, we may link it with the instinct to flee— "flight"— in the face of danger. But rashness is also a vice, in this case an excess associated with spiritedness. This vice we may link with the instinct to "fight" in the face of danger. But one can be too spirited as well as too frightened. Soldiers may rush impulsively into the fray, "blind to the dangers that await them."[14] "Right reason" moderates fear, and courage emerges as fear tempered by spirit.

Aristotle's assignation of courage to the battlefield is far too restrictive for our purposes. The situations where we are called on to be courageous are ever present and various. One does not have to think of graphic cases like the decisions faced by the rescue workers who chose to enter the World Trade Center, knowing full well that they might not come out alive. Courage is also displayed in the familiar domains of every day sickness and death. These domains are also "bat-tlefields" of sorts in which individuals face handicap, major surgery, debilitating illness, and prolonged and painful dying. Think of a situation where a patient and her family must de-cide whether to opt for a risky surgical procedure, or where a physician, by nature and training inclined to take whatever steps are necessary to preserve life, must decide whether to recommend the termination of life-support. Or think of the husband faced with the excruciating decision whether to allow the organs of his brain-dead wife to be used for implantation in others. Aristotle's ethics-of-virtue may prove helpful in all such circumstances. While the theory does not provide hard-and-fast rules to answer the moral questions raised in such instances, it does provide us with a powerful question which can give us some of the guidance we seek. We should not ask: "What should I do?" but rather "What kind of person do I wish to **be** when faced with such circumstances?" Do I wish, for example, to be cowardly, cringing in fear in the face of death, demanding that everything conceivable be done to prolong my life or the life of a loved one, regardless of the quality of life preserved? Do I wish to be one who cringes at the prospect of my loved one's organs being removed, and on this basis declines a request for donation, when I know that great good can come of such donation? Are these options which would be pursued by the person of courage? Is this how "the person of practical wisdom would act," lacking in regard for others, insensitive to the fact that my loved one's organs, or the resources used to prolong her existence when she is in a persistent vegetative state, would be of far greater benefit to others? Or do I want to be courageous, moderating my fear of death, disfigurement, and my insensitivity towards the needs of others as much as it lies within me to do so? To these questions I may find reasonable answers, even if there are no rules by which they can be determined, and even if I must in the end still choose for myself that course of action which best exemplifies the virtuous mean.

The second virtue upon which Aristotle focuses is temperance, which moderates our appetites for things like food, drink, and sexual activity. One can eat too little or too much food. Aristotle designates health as the goal of eating.

Gluttons are guilty of excess. They live to eat rather than eat to live. They imperil rather than preserve their health by over-eating. This is a vice of excess. The vice of defect or deficiency involves eating insufficient food in circumstances where there is enough to go around. In time of scarcity and famine, failure to eat sufficient food is not morally blameworthy. Strictly speaking, in such circumstances eating insufficient food does not even qualify as voluntary action for which assessments of moral praise and blame are appropriate. But in times of plenty, the failure to eat sufficient food to maintain one's health constitutes the vice of deficiency. Although Aristotle does not mention it, malnutrition can presumably also be caused by eating the wrong foods, not just by failing to eat enough food. One can be malnourished on a diet of soda pop and nacho chips, or with fad diets motivated by an inordinate preoccupation with body image. In such cases, Aristotle would attribute malnutrition to vice rather than misfortune or famine.

To be clear on Aristotle's ordering of values in this context, it must be borne in mind that while health is an immediate end of eating, it is not good in itself. Rather it is a means to happiness or well-being, i.e., **eudaemonia**, and is properly conceived only in this way. Relative to moderation in partaking of food and drink, health is a proximate end, but relative to the final end, happiness, it is usually a necessary means. This last point must be kept clearly in mind, particularly in health care contexts where there is sometimes a tendency to confuse means with ends. Life and "health" are important ends of human action, including the actions of health care professionals, but only if, and to the extent that, they contribute to what really counts: **eudaemonia**. When they do not, the person of practical reason and virtue will no longer see them as worthy of pursuit. The implications of this point for decisions concerning the "saving" of people who judge their lives no longer worth living are apparent and profound. Life and "health" are goods which confer rightness on the means for their achievement, but only when these contribute to **eudaemonia**. The belief that human life must be preserved at all costs, regardless of circumstances, would be rejected by Aristotle as mistaken because it confuses means with ends.

An Adequate Theory?

What, in the end, are we to say of Aristotle's virtue theory? As compared with the obligation theories of Kant, Mill and Ross, Aristotle's account of moral life can be seen to have both strengths and weaknesses. Some of these we have already encountered. First, the strengths.

Strengths

One strength of Aristotle's virtue ethics is that it may better reflect the way in which we approach moral questions. Many times our question is not: "What should I do in these circumstances?" but "What kind of person do I want to be?" "Do I want to be the kind of person who can do this?" Sometimes, of course, we do want an answer to the first question. But it is equally true that we often try to answer that question by first addressing the second and third questions. Do I want to be the kind of person who could let his fear determine his conduct? Do I want to be the kind of person who would be labelled dishonest or untrustworthy? In answering these questions, which Aristotle places front and centre, we quite often discover what we should do in a particular set of circumstances. Of course what Donna decides she ought to do, in order to be courageous, may not be what Greg decides he must do in the same set of circumstances. But this may not, as we have seen, be a sign of weakness in Aristotle's theory. Our moral experience hints at the possibility that there may often be no right answers to moral questions, only reasonable ones, i.e., different answers upon which reasonable people of good will and moral integrity—who display **phronesis**—may settle. That it reflects this aspect of our moral lives better than, say utilitarianism, may in fact be a strength of Aristotle's moral theory. Why engage in the fruitless pursuit of right answers if, as Aristotle held, "precision is not to be sought alike in all discussions. We must be content, in speaking of such subjects [as morality and ethical theory], to indicate the truth roughly and in outline."[15]

A second possible advantage of Aristotle's virtue ethics is that it seems to take better account of the importance we place on **motivation** in the moral assessment of actions and persons. Theories such as Kant's and Mill's which focus on providing tests of right action are sometimes criticized for ignoring the motivations people have in doing what they do. If one is to be a moral person, is it enough to abide by Kant's categorical imperative? Is it enough to make sure that one maximizes utility? Perhaps not. How would we judge Katherine who, out of some abstract sense of moral duty, always tried to act in accordance with the Categorical Imperative? What if Katherine doesn't actually care about people at all? She is just concerned with "doing her duty." Would we not (at least most of us) judge Katherine to be in some sense deficient as a moral person? Or consider Dave who, out of an equally abstract sense of moral duty to all rational creatures, shows no more concern for his children than he does for total strangers. He is, in respect of his children and other people, "strictly impartial as a disinterested benevolent spectator."[16] Would we not also judge Dave to be in some way deficient or less worthy, as compared with another person, Liz, whose motivations spring from love for her children?[17] Generally speaking, most of us wish to be Liz, not Dave. We wish to be, and be associated with, persons whose actions are motivated by kindness, generosity, courage and the like, as opposed to those who "just follow the rules." If so, then Aristotle's virtue theory, which focussed on such virtues and the motivations integral to their cultivation and sustainability may well reflect an aspect of moral life which is marginalized by the alternative theories. Such theories focus on tests of right action and at best view moral motivation as of secondary importance. Motivation may count, but only as a means of ensuring that we always "do the right thing." In the case of Kant, motivation does matter in assessing the moral worth of actions — only actions done from a pure sense of moral duty have unconditional moral worth. But it is far from clear that Kant seized on the right motivation.

A third possible strength of Aristotle's theory is that it can easily accommodate a feature of moral assessment which may be underplayed by utilitarian theories and inconsistent with Kant's Categorical Imperative. Moral assessment is often not an "on or off" thing. That is, in many cases there is not just one and only one action which is morally **right** — with all the others being **wrong**. Rather, the morality of actions sometimes comes in **degrees**. Some actions are morally better or worse than others, with no one action being "the right thing to do." It makes perfectly good sense to say that some forms of conduct are **more courageous** or **more unjust** than others; and Aristotle's virtue ethics seems easily to account for this feature of moral life. It allows us not only to grade conduct as right or wrong; it provides us with a vocabulary in which we can assess actions as morally better or worse.

In fairness, it should be noted that Mill hints at recognition of this fact about moral assessment: that it is not an all or nothing thing. When he introduces us to his principle of utility, Mill does not, in fact, say that the principle of utility judges the right action to be that which maximizes utility. Rather, he says that "[T]he creed which accepts as the foundation of morals "utility" or "the greatest happiness principle" holds that actions are right **in proportion as they tend to promote happiness, wrong as they tend to produce the reverse of happiness**."[18] This suggests that actions can be judged not only in terms of **whether** they maximize utility, but in terms of the **extent** to which they promote utility. And this suggests that some actions can be morally better or worse than others. Regardless, it was Mill's belief that there is (usually) a right action, namely that which maximizes utility, and it is our obligation to perform that action. With Aristotle's theory, however, things are different. When judging conduct in terms of the virtues they display, all we may be able to say is that some actions are more courageous or more generous than others and that we must try to aim at a reasonable mean between excesses.

Weaknesses

The most troublesome weakness of Aristotle's account was earlier identified as one of its greatest strengths: its inability to answer all our moral questions for us. What if this is not a strength but a weakness? True, our moral life is often complex and reasonable people will disagree about what should be done in particular sets of circumstances. There may in some cases be no right answer to a moral question, even when people agree on how to go about discovering it. In terms of descriptive adequacy, any ethical theory which in some way acknowledges this feature of moral life is, to that extent, better than one which minimizes its importance or ignores it entirely. Yet descriptive adequacy is not the only goal of a good ethical theory. A second goal of ethical theory is to help us sort out what we should do, particularly in those cases where reasonable people disagree with one another in ways that really seem to matter, or where they simply cannot figure out what they should be doing. Do we not want our ethical theories to help us out in these situations where we need guidance? Do we not want our theories to guide us, so far as this is possible, to correct moral decision about what we ought to be doing? To be sure, it may be useful to tell the President that he should attempt, when faced with the terrorist threat to crash the airliner, to be courageous, just and compassionate. It may be useful to tell him to act as "a person of practical wisdom," whose actions tend towards a mean between excess and deficiency. But how exactly does a person of practical wisdom display these virtues when faced with the President's dilemma? How does one balance these virtues against one another in such a context? What exactly **is** the golden mean in this kind of case? Of course the President's case is a highly unusual one which most people will never have to face. But there are many other, less dramatic, cases in which equally puzzling questions arise. How does a person of practical wisdom choose to display virtue when dealing with his friends and loved ones? How does he balance virtues like caring and loyalty to one's children, against a virtue like justice? Does there come a point where I must give money to my neighbour Tom so that his children, but not mine, get their new school clothes?[19] Much as in Ross's theory, Aristotle's account may leave us to our own devices just at the point where we need guidance most. It may reflect our current state better than theories which oversimplify or ignore the complexity of moral questions. But surely there is merit in attempting to fashion a theory which can help us to overcome our (current) state of perplexity and indecision.

Perhaps the answer to the above concerns about incompleteness is not that we should reject Aristotle's insights entirely, but that we need to supplement his account of moral virtue with a theory of right action (or obligation) such as one sees articulated in Mill or Kant. In actual fact, displaying virtue in one's life seems, to a very large extent, to be a matter of **following the right principles for the right reasons.**[20] If so, then perhaps the conclusion to be drawn at this point is not that Mill, Kant and Ross are right and Aristotle is wrong, but that, in the words of Mill himself, the "conflicting doctrines, instead of one being true and the other false, share the truth between them, and the non-conforming opinion is needed to supply the remainder of the truth of which the [other] doctrine embodies only a part."[21]

Notes

1. Leslie Stephen, *The Science of Ethics* (New York: G.P. Putnam's Sons, 1882), 155, 158.

2. It will be recalled that Aquinas adopted this (and other) aspects of Aristotle's account of virtue, suggesting that one of the tasks of human law is the cultivation of the appropriate habits associated with virtuous conduct. See Chapter 4 above.

3. Aristotle, *Nicomachean Ethics* (henceforth *NE*), trans. J.L. Ackrill (New York: Humanities Press, 1973), 1094a 1-3.

4. Some take this to be a serious defect of Aristotle's theory. If morality is concerned with what is good for **human beings**, then where does this leave animals, and perhaps even the environment? Indeed, as we shall see below, some think that Aristotle's conception of the good marginalizes even women by, in effect, equating the good with the natural. For according to feminists the "natural" is, in fact, often equated with that which serves the interests of dominant males.

5. *NE*, 1095a 16-20.

6. *NE*, 1106b 36-1107a 2.

7. William Frankena, *Ethics*, 2nd ed. (Englewood Cliffs: Prentice-Hall, 1973), 63.

8. *NE*, 1112a 16-17.

9. *NE*, 1113b 20.

10. St. Thomas Aquinas adopted this aspect of Aristotle's teleological conception of the universe and fashioned an entire theory of natural law upon it. For further details of how an Aristotelean conception of the universe was used by Aquinas to derive moral laws, see Chapter 4 above.

11. Again, see Chapter 4 above where an examination is made of Aquinas' attempt to reconcile the claim that there is a universally binding natural law with the fact of variable moral practices and beliefs.

12. These themes are further explored in Chapter 10.

13. In seeking guidance, perhaps the President could look to the decisions of other world leaders faced with similar choices. For example, he might look to Abraham Lincoln who had to decide whether to embark on a civil war knowing full well that his decision would result in the death of countless men, women and children. Or he might consider Winston Churchill's decision whether to commit his nation to fighting, with similar consequences, the seemingly insurmountable forces of Naziism.

14. *NE*, 1116b 37.

15. *NE*, 1094b 12, 18.

16. John Stuart Mill, *Utilitarianism*, (New York: Bobbs Merrill, 1957), 22.

17. Kant is notorious for claiming that a morally worthy action is one which is done solely from duty, i.e., because it complies with the Categorical Imperative. Any other motives, such as sympathy, benevolence or love, in some way diminish the moral value of the action taken. This view of moral worthiness is no doubt at odds with the views of most people.

18. *Utilitarianism*, 10 (emphasis added).

19. Tom's case is discussed in some detail in Chapter 6 above.

20. Recall our earlier observation that virtue requires **principled** decisions.

21. Mill, *On Liberty*, Shields edn. (Indianapolis: Bobbs-Merrill, 1956), 56.

Ten
Feminist Ethics

A Rejection of "Traditional Ethical Theory"

Many contemporary women and men find all the approaches to morality outlined in the preceding chapters to be in many respects unsatisfactory and alienating. These theories were developed by men who, it is argued, inadvertently brought to bear upon their theoretical positions a number of biases and ways of viewing the world which skew the results of their analyses. Traditional ethical theories simply do not include or take account of the experiences of women, and thus cannot do justice to the moral concerns and experiences of women. More than that, they serve to rationalize and support beliefs and practices which subordinate women; in short, they perpetuate a system of patriarchy. In the view of most feminist ethicists, then, traditional theories "do not constitute the objective, impartial theories that they are claimed to be; rather, most theories reflect and support explicitly gender-biased and often blatantly misogynist values."[1]

Some History

Modern feminist theory starts with history. Throughout history, as feminists have pointed out, men have largely been the ones to occupy positions of power, influence and prestige. They have, in particular, dominated the **public sphere** of human activity, and have brought to this sphere their decidedly male perspective on life. In the view of many feminists, this is a perspective which glorifies power, advantage, "reason over passion" and conflict. Our legal and political institutions have largely been controlled by such men, as have our economic markets. International relations and disputes have traditionally been determined by governments and military institutions which are, by and large, dominated by men. And the results have been less than desirable: unending dispute, conflict, domination, insensitivity to the plight of the less fortunate, and ultimately war. In the view of some feminists, we have not come as far from Hobbes' state of nature as we would like to think.[2]

History teaches us a further lesson, according to many feminists. In virtually all societies throughout history, women's activities have, with few exceptions, been confined to the **private sphere** of home and family. Women have been the main ones to raise children and attend to the domestic front. Attempts to somehow combine a women's domestic responsibilities with activities in the public sphere have, traditionally, been both frowned upon and largely unsuccessful. Consider this example. Up till the mid-point of the twentieth century it was not at all uncommon for women teachers and nurses in many North American jurisdictions to be required, often legally, to relinquish their posts upon entering marriage. A woman was begrudgingly allowed a role in the public sphere (of health care and the public education of children) but only till such time as her responsibilities within the private sphere of the matrimonial home kicked into place. A women's place was the home, and within that private sphere there were certain activities—maintaining the home, rearing children—for which she was thought to be naturally suited and both socially and morally responsible.

To many people the roles, responsibilities and expectations endorsed by this traditional view of women are "natural" and unobjectionable. The social role of women, it is claimed, is dictated by God, or by certain unalterable biological and psychological facts about men and women: only women can bear children and breast feed infants; women are more caring and nurturing than men; women are naturally more emotional and less rational than men. The latter is shown in their stronger emotional ties to their children and their comparative inability, attested to by many leading philosophers like Aristotle and Aquinas, to make rational decisions or to reason theoretically. According to this traditional view these so-called truths of biology and psychology are obvious and unalterable. In the view of natural law theorists like Aquinas they are all part of God's Eternal Law, the "plan of government in the Chief Governor."[3] They also fit together to justify the conclusion that women are naturally suited for the role of wife, mother, and homemaker, and unsuited for roles within the public sphere of law, politics and commerce.

Yet another key element of this traditional picture of women is the claim that women have not in any way been disadvantaged by accepting the social roles for which biology and psychology make them suitable. According to this view, it is in these roles that a woman finds personal fulfilment and meaning in her life; women have willingly accepted, indeed chosen, their place in the social structure, prompted by their natural inclination towards motherhood and nurturing. And they have found that their natural place in society brings its own kind of power and influence—different from that of men, but no less effective in achieving what women really want from their lives.

Feminists reject this picture of women and their role within society. According to virtually all feminists there is nothing natural or biologically pre-ordained about such arrangements. Furthermore, women do not freely choose to be confined to the private sphere. Rather, that choice is imposed upon women by a society whose levers of power are held by men who enforce, most notably through legal sanction but also through powerful moral and social sanction, the traditional roles and expectations of women. It is true, feminists argue, that only women can (at least for the time being) bear or breastfeed children, but these biological facts do not determine that it is women who must bear the burden, or even most of the burden, of rearing children. Nor do they imply that women should be precluded from full participation in the public sphere. Aristotle and Aquinas notwithstanding, there is nothing natural about restricting women to the private sphere of home and hearth. The "natural" is in reality only the traditional or conventional—and traditions and conventions can be changed.

Patriarchy and the Subjugation of Women

According to modern feminists the subordination of women is not, despite rhetoric suggesting otherwise, a thing of the past. Nor is it restricted to the many highly traditional, theocratic societies in existence today—societies in which women are prevented from voting, showing their faces in public, or even driving cars. In the view of most feminists even our western democratic societies continue to be dominated by men. Indeed, they are **structured** in the interests of men and against the interests of women. The term **patriarchy** is used by feminists to refer to the type of society rationalized by the "traditional" picture of women sketched above. Patriarchy, as understood by feminists, involves the **systematic subordination of women in the interests of men.** This phenomenon is, feminists believe, pervasive. It's reflected in our laws, our social customs, and our personal expectations. Most importantly, for our purposes, it is reflected in our moral beliefs and practices, and our traditional ethical theories.

In the view of all feminists, patriarchy should be eliminated from all facets of our societies. And we are, feminists claim, quite capable of bringing this about, so long as we are willing to challenge deeply embedded ways of doing and thinking about things. Feminists are united in rejecting patriarchy. As contemporary feminist philosopher Patricia Smith puts it: "Feminists think that patriarchy (the subjugation of women) is not good, not ordained by nature, and not inevitable."[4]

Feminist approaches to ethics, then, all share some central principles—notably a desire to correct various forms of male bias in the study of ethics. But they do not share the same approach, or all come to the same conclusions. Some argue on the basis of rights, some on utilitarian, consequentialist grounds, some on the grounds of virtue ethics; some focus on women as a whole; some on the issues of race or class or sexual orientation that make the experiences of some groups of women quite different from those of others. Many link ethics with epistemology, suggesting that the male-dominated field of western philosophy has tended to rely too heavily on certain approaches to knowledge and to devalue others that are inherently no less useful. And there are vast differences too in matters of style. Many feminist moral philosophers (such as Alison Jaggar, Susan Sherwin, and Rosemarie Tong[5]) write from within the mainstream of Western analytic philosophy even while challenging many of its presumptions. Others (such as Luce Irigaray, Julia Kristeva, and Mary Daly) adopt a much looser style that draws both on the non-analytic traditions of Continental philosophy and on the traditions of other disciplines such as literary study.

One of the core issues on which there is a wide divergence of feminist views is the issue of whether or not there are virtues or values that are particularly to be associated with women. Many feminists today argue that the tendency of women to be attracted towards the "helping professions" is a social construct that deserves to be discarded. They are profoundly skeptical of any effort to treat virtues such as a propensity towards caring as inherently feminine, arguing that such an endeavour plays into the hands of those who prefer to keep women in traditional roles.

It would be impossible to provide a complete and fully accurate account of the important, multi-faceted themes pursued by feminist ethicists. Instead, we will attempt in what follows to sketch a few of the major themes that have emerged in recent years within the feminist literature. These themes revolve around the question whether there is such a thing as a decidedly "feminine nature" and whether a distinctly "feminine ethics" (in particular, a feminine "ethics of care") can be based upon it. Although in no way exhaustive of the full range of meta-ethical and normative positions adopted by feminist writers, these questions form an important touchstone in much feminist discourse about ethics. As such they provide a useful first focal point for further discussion of the full range of feminist perspectives in ethical theory. They will therefore be the focus for much of our discussion in this chapter.

A Feminine Nature?

The idea that women are radically different in nature from men is not a new one. As noted earlier, philosophers such as Aristotle and Kant believed that women were less rational than men and that important decisions, particularly those within the public sphere, should therefore be left to men. According to Kant, a woman's passionate nature prevents her from rising to a level of moral development at which she can properly ask the question demanded by the Categorical Imperative: "Can I consistently will, as a universal law of nature, the maxim of my action?" According to Kant, women are ill equipped by nature to answer such an abstract, rational question. Jean Jacques Rousseau suggested in **Emile** that women's different natures entail that different virtues are applicable to them, those integral to their natural roles as wives and mothers. Rousseau wanted to insist that a woman's nature, roles and virtues are in no way inferior to man's, just different. But as many modern feminists have stressed, thinking of men and women as different in nature has led to the subordination of women. In particular, it has led to the restriction of women to the private sphere. And this, in turn, has had the effect (intentional or otherwise) of denying them influence within the ever powerful public domain. The result is subjugation, even if the intention is to idealize women and the "womanly virtues." Viewing women as "different but equal" can be as dangerous as adopting social policies which licence "separate but equal" treatment of racial minorities.[6]

Almost all feminist ethicists share this sort of concern about seeing women's nature as essentially different from that of men; no feminist philosopher defends the nineteenth-century position that women and men are biologically predisposed towards different ethical virtues and vices. Some feminist ethicists do, however, suggest that divergent ethical tendencies exist as a result of social constructs; such constructs are not biologically determined, but they may nevertheless be quite real in their operation in the here and now.

Underlying this discussion is the distinction between "sex" and "gender," which has become a fundamental conceptual tool within feminism. Whereas a person's sex is a biological category, pertaining to chromosomes, hormones, and anatomical features, a person's gender is largely or entirely[7] constructed at the social or cultural level. As Simone de Beauvoir, the French existentialist philosopher put it in **The Second Sex** (perhaps the most influential feminist work of the twentieth century), "One is not born, but becomes a woman. No biological, psychological, or economic fate determines the figure that the human female presents in society: it is civilization as a whole that produces this creature...which is described as feminine."[8] Our notions of what constitutes an attractive male or female appearance, what constitutes "masculine" or "feminine" behaviour, and what roles may be appropriate for women and for men—all these are generated by the culture in which we live. So too, many claim, are many of the ways in which we tend to approach social situations or ethical problems.

It is from the perspective of gender, then, that some contemporary feminist thinkers have suggested that, in general, women do bring a decidedly different perspective and way of thinking to moral questions and that we can profit by developing a distinctive feminist ethics based on this perspective. Whether the aim is to replace the traditional ethical theories with a new alternative, or simply to supplement those theories with insights ignored by those (patriarchal) theories, the claim is that we can advance our moral practices and theories by considering the "feminine" perspective on morality.

Kohlberg and Gilligan

In her groundbreaking book, **In A Different Voice: Psychological Theory and Women's Development**, Carol Gilligan advanced the thesis that women and men do in fact tend to reason differently about moral questions.[9] Gilligan's conclusions arose from her critical study of Lawrence Kohlberg's theories on the moral development of children.[10] Kohlberg argued that children advance through six distinct stages of moral reasoning, beginning with an initial stage where right action is viewed as submitting to the authority of others with the power to inflict punishment on them, and culminating in the final stage of moral development where they are able to consider and apply abstract universal rules and principles of morality. This final stage is, Kohlberg suggested, the distinctly moral stage where full moral agency is apparent. In between are stages where the morality of one's action is thought to be determined by factors like social roles, fidelity to friends, family and partners, and so on. At these intermediate stages, there is more emphasis on special relationships and individuating circumstances, as opposed to the abstract, universal principles contemplated at the sixth and final level of development.

In developing his theory, Kohlberg relied on children's responses to questions concerning a moral dilemma. Gilligan used the questions constructed by Kohlberg in conducting her own psychological studies, but came to a radically different analysis of the responses. The most frequently discussed example of Gilligan's experiments involved two 11 year-old

children, Jake and Amy, who were asked how they would re-
spond to the following moral dilemma.

> Heinz's wife is dying but the pharmacist who is selling
> the drug which will save her life is charging a wildly
> inflated price. Heinz cannot afford the $2000 asking
> price, but he can come up with $1000. Even at this
> lower price the pharmacist stands to make a very large
> profit. Both Heinz's offer to buy the drug at the lower
> price, and his offer to pay $1000 now and a further
> $1000 later, are rejected by the pharmacist. Heinz is
> now in a dilemma: should he steal the drug to save his
> wife?

Jake had no doubt that, morally speaking, Heinz should steal
the drug. In coming to this firm conclusion he utilized rules
having to do with property and the value of life. Amy, on the
other hand, responded very differently. She suggested that
Heinz should not steal the drug—there were, to her way of
thinking, other avenues to be explored. He should try to talk
things out with the druggist, or find some other way of getting
the money to pay him. In Amy's mind Heinz and the druggist
should try to find a mutually satisfactory resolution to the
problem. Jake looked for answers in abstract principles governing property and the value of human lives; Amy looked for
solutions through mediation, communication, compromise
and the personal relationship between Heinz and the druggist. Under Kohlberg's model, Amy had not ascended to the
more advanced stage of moral reasoning Jake had attained.
Her moral development was less advanced than Jake's.

According to Gilligan, Kohlberg drew the wrong conclusions from his studies of children like Jake and Amy. The
two children do reason differently about Heinz's case, but

Amy's response is in no way inferior or less advanced than Jake's. Amy's response was identified by Gilligan as more typical of women, whereas Jake's was identified as more typical of men.[11] Amy attempted to resolve the dilemma by an approach which emphasizes communication, compromise, caring, special attention to concrete details, and the various personal relationships and emotional bonds involved. She appealed to what many feminist philosophers now call an "ethics of care." Jake, on the other hand, emphasized logical reasoning and abstract, impartial and universal principles. The latter approach, Gilligan suggested, is not superior. Indeed, it misses out on a good deal of what actually concerns people in their everyday moral lives. This "ethics of abstract, universal principle" ignores the roles played by special relationships, emotional bonds, discussion, and compromise in our everyday moral lives. It misses out on an important fact well recognized by most women, and now by many advocates of feminist ethics generally: that a good deal of our moral lives are concerned with the particular personal relationships we share with others. Personal, caring relationships, with all their individuality, subtlety and complexity, are the cornerstones of our moral lives. It seriously distorts the role of these relationships if we conceive them as governed by abstract principle—if we think of ourselves as being guided by such standards in living lives structured by these relationships. By ignoring particularized, caring relationships, and instead elevating the ethics of abstract principle to an exalted status, both Kohlberg and traditional ethical theory have simply ignored or distorted fundamental aspects of moral life.

Here it should be emphasized that Gilligan presents paradigms that she associates with gender as it has been constructed in Western society; she does not suggest that the different tendencies she identifies are inherently to be associated with female and male. Indeed, in the introduction to the revised edition of her groundbreaking work she laments the way in which her work has sometimes been misinterpreted: "When I hear my work being cast in terms of whether women and men are really (essentially) different or who is better than whom, I know that I have lost my voice, because these are not my questions."[12]

An Ethics of Principle versus An Ethics of Care

Feminist philosophers such as Nel Noddings have advanced an alternative view that gives emotional response a place of central importance in the ethical world. According to Noddings, ethical action is caring action; an action "is right or wrong according to how faithfully it is rooted in caring."[13] Feminists such as Noddings share Gilligan's rejection of abstract, universalizable principles and rules as the way of answering everyone's moral questions. The theories of Kant and Mill are often cited as illustrative of the vacuousness, indeed the perniciousness, of traditional ethical theory. In the view of his feminist critics Kant rejects the emotional, personal component of moral life in favour of the rational universalizability of individual maxims. In seeking rationally to universalize our maxims, we are inescapably led to ignore or submerge our concern for all those complex factors, some non-rational, which individuate our situations and the relationships in which we find ourselves. Most importantly perhaps, in seeking such abstractions we are led to ignore, or abstract away, all that makes us individual persons enmeshed in inter-personal relationships involving caring and trust. Among the factors so eliminated are the emotional bonds between people and the special concerns they have for one another as parents, friends, siblings, and colleagues.[14] In seeking to universalize we are, it is claimed, led to forget that most of the time we approach one another—and believe ourselves morally right in doing so—not as strangers subject to the same set of universalized maxims or rights, but as unique individuals in highly personal, context-specific relationships in which we have much invested emotionally. These are relationships which, by their very nature, cannot be reduced to universalized rules and principles. According to one leading feminist ethicist:

> Because women are usually charged with the responsibility of caring for children, the elderly, and the ill as well as the responsibility of physically and emotionally nurturing men, both at work and at home, most women experience the world as a complex web of interdependent relationships, where responsible caring for others is implicit in their moral lives. The abstract reasoning of morality that centres on the rights [and duties] of independent agents is inadequate for the moral reality in which they live. Most women find that a different model for ethics is necessary; the traditional ones are not persuasive.[15]

A Valid Indictment?

Despite the undoubted insights generated by this feminist critique of mainstream ethical theory, one may reasonably ask whether its condemnation of the ethics of principle is fully justified. It is no doubt true that both women and men experience the world as a complex web of personal relationships often cemented by emotional bonds and responsible caring. Any theory which denies or ignores these features of moral life is clearly inadequate. It may also be true that, given their traditional social roles, women have become more attuned to these important dimensions of moral life. Furthermore, there is little doubt that the circumstances of everyday life are often complex, multi-faceted, variable and not easily amenable to assessment by very abstract universal rules. But now comes a crucial question: Does all this mean that we must reject theories which would have us appeal to principles, rules, and the **universalizability** of moral judgments? Does this mean, in short, that we must abandon the ethics of principle altogether in favour of some other form of ethical theory?

One should be careful in answering these questions in the affirmative. Perhaps the experiences of women do lead them to value personal relationships, particularly ones involving the care of others, more than men do. But the conclusion to be drawn from this may not be that we should abandon appeals to principles completely and focus on particular relationships of care. Rather, the conclusion to be drawn may be that the situations of most women lead them to have different priorities than men, to rank their principles—including those involved in personal (and sometimes caring) relationships—differently from men. One might reasonably ask what is lost if caring relationships are understood in terms of **principles** of care. If the answer is that relationships are personal, particular and individuated and therefore not amenable to governance by principle, then there are a number of responses to be made.

First, every act, event, person, indeed every **thing** is, in some important sense, particular and individual. That this is so does not prevent us from abstracting from these particularities and conceiving of the world as composed of **categories** or **types** of things. Stella and Carmelle are unique individuals, but that does not prevent us from thinking of them as human persons, women, mothers, employees, Catholics, sisters, and so on. In some instances, of course, it would be a mistake to think of Stella and Carmelle in terms of their similarities and to ignore their differences entirely. Many injustices are the result of such failures to observe relevant differences among people.[16] But it would equally be a mistake, in other situations, to stress their differences and ignore their similarities. It would be a mistake, in making a decision about vacation entitlement, to ignore the fact that Stella and Carmelle have similar work experiences, seniority and performance evaluations. The same is true of virtually all situations giving rise to moral questions. We may share certain special, and in many ways unique, relationships with others; and these individuating features may in some instances make an important difference when it comes to assessing our moral responsibilities. But whatever our relationships and particular circumstances might be, they will be at least partially definable and understandable as the instantiations of general types.

We do well, in this context, to remember an important point raised earlier in Chapter 7 where we looked at what it is to act on a maxim of action, i.e., to act on the basis of **reasons** for action. As noted there, giving reasons for what we do inevitably involves **universalizability**. If I put forward R as a sufficient reason for me to do X, then logical consistency commits me to saying that R is a sufficient reason for anyone else in a situation like mine. And this includes situations where I stand in some special relationship with someone else. If the fact that **my** children will suffer disadvantage if I give Tom the money for his kid's new school clothes provides a sufficient reason for **me** to spend it on my own kids, then I commit myself to saying that this is true of any parent in a situation like mine. It would be wrong for me to make an exception for my kids if I am not prepared to extend the same exception to other similarly situated people. And this involves me in thinking not just of **my** situation, but the **kind** or **type** of situation in which I find myself. Yet once we have begun to think in terms of general kinds or types of actions, persons, events and so on, we have begun to think in ways that are amenable to assessment by **universal** standards like rules and principles. A recognition of the importance of context, then, need not lead us to abandon the ethics of principle entirely.

The Universal and the General

If the above is true, then one might reasonably ask "Why is there such a firm reaction among many feminists[17] and some other critics of traditional ethical theory to the ethics of principle, and more generally to the idea that moral judgments are universalizable, that is, subject to universal standards of appraisal?" One reason may be a common failure to observe an important distinction between two distinct properties: the **universal** and the **general**. A general rule or principle is one which applies to a wide variety of different kinds of situations. Consider the following two rules:

> R1: All vehicles must observe a 60 km per hour speed limit.

> R2: All four-wheel drive sport utility vehicles must observe a 60 km per hour speed limit within city limits.

R1 is a much more general rule than R2. It applies to a wider variety of different kinds of situations and vehicles. Unlike R2, it applies to two-wheel drive vehicles, vans, transport trucks, and so on. It also applies both inside and outside city limits. However, although R1 and R2 differ in the degree of generality, they are equally universal in application. They apply equally to **all** members of the general class of things to which they make reference. R1 applies to **all** vehicles; R2 applies to **all** four-wheel drive, SUVs within city limits.[18]

With this distinction in hand, we are now in a better position, perhaps, to appreciate the complaint of those feminists who object to an ethics of principle. The objection is not to universal principles—i.e., to principles intended to apply to all persons, acts and circumstances within their scope. Rather, the objection is to a tendency to **over-generalize**, to abstract from the particularities of life and ignore all those contextual features which are so important to a proper moral assessment of our conduct. But there is nothing in the theories of Kant, Mill, Ross or Aristotle which would lead us inevitably to ignore these features. Take Mill as our example. If we are to seek the maximization of utility, then it is reasonable to think that we will be led to govern our lives by way of general rules of thumb whose observance leads to the maximization of utility. But if we are to pursue this indirect strategy, then we had better be careful not to overgeneralize. We had better be careful, that is, not to ignore features of the various situations governed by our rules of thumb which might be responsible for different levels of utility. If there are differences in utility between situation 1 and situation 2, then a rule which fails to distinguish between these two situations will not be the best rule.

Let us look again at an example considered above. Recall that my children want new clothes to begin their school year.

The clothes they already have are more than adequate, but each year they derive a certain amount of happiness from beginning the school year with a new set of threads. Down the street lives our widowed, unemployed father, Tom, and his two children. The children have nothing but somewhat tattered summer clothes, and Tom lacks the financial resources to buy new clothing. Furthermore, the three lack the support of an extended family and are ineligible for government assistance. Suppose, now, that I am an advocate of Mill's theory who wishes to consider a rule of thumb to govern such situations. Suppose I accept the general rule, R, that one should devote one's resources to whomever will benefit most from them. As a result, I forgo buying my kids their new clothes so that I can give the money to Tom.

Would I be right in adopting this rule? Must I be **impartial** between the happiness of my children and that of my neighbour's children? Surely not. My rule, R, neglects the special relationships parents—not just **me**, but also **parents like me**—share with their children, special relationships the fostering of which by **all** parents would generally lead to overall gains in utility. So my rule is far too general, even though it is universal in its scope (it applies to anyone with resources to spend on others). R ignores the important differences between cases involving strangers or acquaintances, on the one hand, and those involving loved ones and dependents, on the other. But notice this absolutely crucial point. Any rule that I substitute for R, which requires less than complete impartiality, will be no less universal than R itself. Suppose I adopt a less general rule, R⋆, according to which one should devote a measure of one's resources to helping out strangers and acquaintances so long as this does not result in compromising one's responsibility to care for one's dependents. R⋆, though it is far less general than R, applies to **all** situations in which one is able to commit resources without compromising the special responsibilities one has to one's dependents.

The strands of feminism we have been focusing on in these pages have highlighted the importance of appreciating a range of important differences which arise within particular contexts. If the above reflections are correct, however, it would be a mistake to view them as having established the need to reject the ethics of universal principles altogether. If we continue to maintain the requirement that we always provide reasons for our moral choices, then we inevitably fall back on universalizable judgments and the universal (though not necessarily general) standards upon which these are based.

The Importance of the Wider Context

The feminist concern for the importance of context leads in another direction as well. Many feminists stress not only the importance of appreciating the factors which individuate one case from the other and tie us to one another in a variety of personal ways; such feminists also stress the importance of appreciating the **wider** context of decision-making. This is a context which, more often than not, profoundly influences the options available, or thought available, to us. Feminists have led many to look beyond the individual situations in which decisions are made and to question the social and political institutions, practices, and beliefs that create those situations and define the available options and the concepts in terms of which they are understood.

Consider, for example, the case of reproductive technology. Here a plethora of ethical questions arise whenever a woman requests reproductive assistance in the face of infertility. Should any woman who asks for such aid be accommodated? What if she is unmarried, in a same sex relationship, or already has children of her own? Is it permissible to create multiple fertilized eggs when only a few will actually be implanted at any one time? If so, may some of the extra eggs be used for purposes of medical research, say stem cell research? These questions, and many others like them, are ones which continue to confront us — women in particular — as biomedical technologies develop at an increasingly rapid rate.

But many feminist ethicists want to dig much deeper than the set of questions outlined above would suggest. They want to uncover for discussion the variety of social, political, and environmental factors which give rise to such questions and possibly frame the available answers. They wish to expose certain social factors (mostly products of patriarchy) which arguably lead many women to request treatment despite the negligible chance of success and the profound disappointment which often accompanies failure. Many argue that our conventionally accepted, traditional view of women's social role, as fundamentally including the production and rearing of children, encourages infertile women to conceive of themselves as defective and lacking in value. In coming to accept this conception of themselves, they are in effect "coerced" into seeking biomedical interventions to "correct" themselves. And they suffer great feelings of inadequacy and worthlessness if, as is all too common, such interventions fail to bring about the desired result. Similar points are made in relation to cosmetic surgery, which many claim is often pursued by women only because of the force of socially generated stereotypes of femininity which ground a woman's value in her good looks. Our society has "socially constructed" an image of women's beauty which leads to harmful results. What appear to be free choices, made in the exercise of moral agency, are in reality the products of coercive social forces.

Traditional ethical theory ignores this wider context of moral decision-making and is seriously deficient as a result.

Not all feminist philosophers, it should be emphasized, want to abandon traditional ethical theories. Indeed, a number of important feminist philosophers have focused their energies on turning afresh to traditional ethical theories in an effort to determine what morality requires of us when these theories are consistently and fully applied to both women and men. Among them are Susan Moller Okin, whose pioneering work discusses how to apply traditional theories of justice to women as well as men,[19] and Virginia Held, who has related notions of justice to the concept of care, particularly of children.[20] Several leading philosophers have revisited Kantian philosophy and offered reinterpretations that aim to adequately deal with issues of gender. Annette Baier has drawn on Hume as well as Kant while breaking new ground in virtue theory.[21] Martha Nussbaum, for her part, draws on Aristotelian philosophy in formulating a set of feminist principles that argue strongly for universalizability, and for a global approach.[22] Other feminists too have taken global approaches, with some (such as Vandana Shiva) linking feminism with ecology, others (such as Chandra Mohanty) linking feminism with third world and postcolonial politics. And still others (Julia Kristeva and Judith Butler perhaps most prominent among them) have drawn on the work of the French philosophers Jacques Derrida and Michel Foucault to forge post-structuralist and postmodernist feminist theories.

On balance, then, feminist philosophers have presented a wide range of challenges to traditional ethical theories; even when they have drawn on those theories, they have tended to place ethical discussions in a much wider context than traditional male-dominated ethical theory had been in the habit of doing.

Summing Up

To sum up, many strands of feminist ethics are marked by a rejection of traditional ethical theory on the grounds that it is too abstract and too concerned with universalized rules and principles. As such, traditional ethical theory is said to miss out on two fronts. First, it renders irrelevant a host of individuating factors which inform our moral lives and which most of us, women in particular, consider integral to moral assessment. These include the importance of personal, caring relationships and the emotional bonds that exist between individuals who care for one another. Within these relationships our conduct is (or at least should be) typically marked by attempts to achieve consensus and mutual accommodation. We do not see ourselves as attempting to solve our moral problems by applying moral rules outlining our rights and duties, as traditional ethical theories presuppose. Second, traditional ethical theory is said to ignore the wider social, political, and environmental contexts in which moral questions are shaped and the available options are defined. Whether or not these various indictments of traditional ethical theory are in the end all sustainable, there is no doubt that feminists have led us to a far richer understanding of the complexities of moral life.

Notes

1. Susan Sherwin, "Ethics, 'Feminine Ethics,' and Feminist Ethics," in Debra Shogan (ed.), *A Reader in Feminist Ethics* (Toronto: Canadian Scholar's Press, 1993), 10.

2. See Chapter 5 above for Hobbes' description of the state of nature where life is solitary, poor, nasty, brutish and short.

3. See Chapter 4 above.

4. *Feminist Jurisprudence* (New York: OUP, 1993), p. 3.

5. Tong provides an excellent overview of the various strands of feminism in her *Feminist Theory: A More Comprehensive Introduction* 2nd ed. (Boulder: Westview, 1998).

6. Certain racial groups have, historically, been subjected to discrimination as a result of so-called "separate but equal" treatment. Particularly notable examples are the treatment received by Afro-Americans in the middle of the twentieth century and by South African blacks under apartheid.

7. Some feminist philosophers argue that gender is entirely a social or cultural construct, others that biology and culture jointly construct gender.

8. Simone de Beauvoir, *The Second Sex*, translated by H.M. Parshley (New York: Bantam, 1952; *Le Deuxieme Sexe* originally published 1949), p. 249. The famous first sentence of this passage (in the original French, "On ne naît pas femme, on le devient") is often translated as "Woman is not born, but made."

9. Carol Gilligan, *In A Different Voice: Psychological Theory and Women's Development* (Cambridge: Harvard University Press, 1982).

10. See generally, L. Kohlberg, *The Psychology of Moral Development* (San Francisco: Harper and Row, 1981).

11. It is worth noting here that, quite aside from any differences over the implications of Gilligan's research, its reliability has also been called into question. The conservative scholar Christina Hoff Sommers has been the strongest critic of Gilligan's methodology and failure to make all her data public, but a number of other scholars have also raised doubts about such issues as sample size and choice of question.

12. Carol Gilligan, *In A Different Voice: Psychological Theory and Women's Development* 2nd ed. (Cambridge: Harvard University Press, 1994), 4. The misinterpretations did not stop with the publication of the revised edition, however. In a 1996 Supreme Court case, for example, the state of Virginia argued (United States v. Virginia) that Gilligan's research supported the state's exclusion of women from the Virginia Military Academy; Gilligan filed a brief arguing against what she saw as a serious misrepresentation of her views.

13. Nel Noddings, *Caring: A Feminine Approach to Ethics and Education* (Berkeley: University of California Press, 1984), 53.

14. Ross, of course, stressed such relationships. But, his feminist critics would no doubt argue that he mistakenly conceives these as governed by duties and the rules and principles upon which they are based.

15. Sherwin, "Ethics, 'Feminine Ethics,' and Feminist Ethics," 14.

16. Affirmative action programs are often justified by a tendency to ignore relevant differences between advantaged and disadvantaged groups.

17. A significant number of feminists do in fact defend universalizable accounts of rights and duties (see p. 239).

18. Again, there is absolutely nothing in the notion of a universalized maxim of action which entails that a universalized maxim must be highly abstract or general. And to say (along with both Kant and Hare) that moral judgments must be universalizable, is not to say that one's judgments must apply to everybody indiscriminately. It is only to say that it must apply to **everyone whose situation is similar to the one in which I find myself**.

19. See Susan Moller Okin, *Justice, Gender and the Family* (New York: Basic, 1991).

20. Virginia Held, *Feminist Morality: Transforming Culture, Society, and Politics* (Chicago: University of Chicago Press, 1993).

21. See in particular Annette Baier, *Moral Prejudices: Essays on Ethics* (Cambridge: Harvard University Press, 1994).

22. See in particular Martha Nussbaum, *Sex and Social Justice* (Oxford: Oxford University Press, 1999).

Index

Index

duties. *See also* obligation
of fair play, 156–57, 162
of fidelity, 193
of gratitude, 193–94
of justice, 193
of non-interference, 48
of non-maleficence, 194
plurality of irreducible, 199
of reparation, 193
of self-improvement, 193
Dworkin, Ronald, 103

Emile (Rousseau), 229
emotivism, 20, 29, 59–61, 93n
episteme, 203–4
epistemological questions, 27
equality, 122
Eternal Law, 104–5, 112, 117, 225
ethical pluralism, 189–00
ethical theory
codes of ethics, 20
goal, 220
guide to practice of morality, 14
as philosophical theory, 25
practical and theoretical limits, 211
relation to morality, 13, 25
ethics of care, 228, 233–34, 245n
ethics of principle, 233–36, 239
eudaemonia, 205, 208, 210, 215–16
Euthyphro (Plato), 95

facts, 59
factual beliefs, 79–81, 87
factual disputes, 92
factual questions, 78–79
fairness, 170
principle of, 38
Feinberg, Joel, 45–46
feminist ethics, 117, 120n, 221n, 223–46

concern for context, 241
ethics of care, 228, 233–34, 245n
feminine nature, 228–29
feminine perspective on morality, 231
personal relationships, 236
post-structuralist and postmodernist, 243
Finnis, John, 103
Foucault, Michel, 243
Frankena, William, 206
free riders, 156–57
free will, 105–6
freedom rights, 48–49, 57
protected freedoms, 51
friendliness, 212
friendship, 192
Fuller, Lon, 103
Fundamental Principle (FP), 106–8

Gauthier, David, 123, 128, 139, 196
co-operation, 133
constrained maximization, 130–35
cooperative surplus, 136, 138
minimax relative concession, 135, 137–38
rational choice, 128–29
straightforward utility maximization, 130–31, 133–35, 138
views on practical rationality, 124
gender, 233, 243, 245n
as social and cultural construct, 230
generosity, 212
Gilligan, Carol, 231–34

Index

on women, 229
Kepler, Johannes, 79
knowledge, 41, 148
  practical, 203–4, 211, 217
  theoretical, 203–4
Kohlberg, Lawrence, 231–33
Koorsgaard, Christine, 243
Kristeva, Julia, 228, 243

language of obligation, 63n
language of rights, 42, 44, 53, 55,
  63n
Language Truth and Logic (Ayer),
  59
law, force of, 122, 126
law of non-contradiction, 106,
  119n
legal judgments, 16
legal rights, 45–47
legal sanctions, 226
Leibniz, G.W., 95, 98–100, 103
  "principles of perfection," 97
Leviathan (Hobbes), 125
libertarians, 49, 57
liberties, 50, 125–26
Locke, John, 43, 121
logical consistency, 78, 84–86,
  177–79
logical contradiction, 179–80
  law of non-contradiction, 106,
  119n
loyalty, 192, 212

maximization of utility, 167–68
maxims, 174–77, 179, 182, 185,
  237
mean, 210, 212–13
meaning, 27
meta-ethics, 27, 29
metaphysical, 27
Mill, John Stuart, 21–22, 24, 26–
  29, 39–40, 145–48, 151–53,

190, 202, 216–17, 219, 221.
  See also utilitarianism
duty ethics, 210
feminist criticism of, 234, 239
minimax relative concession,
  135–38
  absolute magnitude, 136
  cooperative surplus, 136
  moderation, 212
Moharty, Chandra, 243
monistic theories of value, 40–42,
  146, 149–50
monistic theory of obligation,
  39–40, 174, 191
Moore, G.E., 22, 41, 148, 190
moral agency, 176, 203, 208, 231
  coercive social forces, 242
moral argumentation, 83
moral beliefs, 80, 227
moral codes, 62
moral commitments, 155, 162
moral conventionalism, 67–68, 70,
  83, 86, 93n–94n, 104, 195
  alleged consequences, 71–75
  cultural conventions, 118
  cultural norms, 29
  culture, 74
moral facts, 59
Moral Ground version, 96–100,
  104
moral ideals. *See* supererogation
moral imperialism, 66, 93n
Moral Index version, 100–103
moral intuition, 20–21, 194–95
moral judgments, 16–18, 21, 81,
  118, 174, 180
  indeterminacy, 211
  justification, 20, 26
  meaning of, 58–63
  as moral sense or sentiment,
  173
  nature and meaning of, 26

Index

passive rights, 46, 48–50
past actions, 155
paternalism, 184
patriarchy, 117, 223, 226–27, 231
phronesis, 203–4, 211, 217
Plato, 95, 103
pleasure, 32, 40–41, 146–52, 205.
    See also happiness
    interpersonal comparison, 41
    of the mind, 147
    physical, 147
pluralistic theories, 39, 41, 148,
    191–92, 211
political authority, 43
political philosophy, 121
positive rights, 46–47, 50, 56–57
powers, 53–55
    of agency, 55
    of consent, 54
    of promising, 55
    of surrogacy, 55
practical knowledge, 203–4, 211,
    217
practical or applied ethics, 29
practical rationality, 123, 132
Preference Utilitarianism, 22, 148
prescriptivism, 61–62
prima facie duties, 192–93, 199
    conflicting, 199
    self-evidence, 194–96
    weighing, 197
Prisoner's Dilemma, 128–32
privacy, 52
privileges, 51–52, 55, 152
    comparison with active freedom
        rights, 50
    as freedom from duty, 50
    unprotected liberties, 53
proairesis, 207–8
professional codes of ethics, 19
progress, 23, 138–39
    reform, 72, 81

promises, 55, 155–56, 165, 169,
    179, 191–92
    false, 180
prudence, 73, 78, 119, 126–27,
    132. *See also* self-interest
    judgment of, 17–18, 21

rational choice, 128–29
rationality, 105, 186
    practical, 123, 132
Rawls, John, 166–67
reason, 73, 82, 105–6, 111–12,
    118, 173, 213. *See also* moral
    reasoning
    over passion, 224
    practical, 211
    sufficient reason, 175–76
reasons, 18, 177, 184, 237, 241
    good reasons, 74
relativism. *See* Moral Relativism
reproductive technology, 241
right reason. *See under* Kant,
    Immanuel
rights, 43, 202, 227
    claim-rights, 45–56, 64n
    freedom rights, 48–51, 57
    language of, 42, 44, 53, 55, 63n
    legal rights, 45–47
    liberties, 50, 125–26
    moral, 45–47
    natural, 43, 126
    negative rights, 46–51, 56–57
    passive rights, 46, 48–50
    in personam rights, 46, 50, 56
    positive rights, 46–47, 50,
        56–57
    in rem rights, 46–47, 50, 56
    security rights, 49–50
    talk, 42–44, 55
    terminology of, 38
Roe v Wade, 56

From the Publisher

A name never says it all, but the word "Broadview" expresses a good deal of the philosophy behind our company. We are open to a broad range of academic approaches and political viewpoints. We pay attention to the broad impact book publishing and book printing has in the wider world; for some years now we have used 100% recycled paper for most titles. Our publishing program is internationally oriented and broad-ranging. Our individual titles often appeal to a broad reader-ship too; many are of interest as much to general readers as to academics and students.

Founded in 1985, Broadview remains a fully independent company owned by its shareholders—not an imprint or subsidiary of a larger multinational.

For the most accurate information on our books (including information on pricing, editions, and formats) please visit our website at www.broadviewpress.com. Our print books and ebooks are also available for sale on our site.

broadview press
www.broadviewpress.com

This book is made of paper from well-managed FSC® - certified forests, recycled materials, and other controlled sources.

FSC
www.fsc.org
MIX
Paper from responsible sources
FSC® C103567

PCF

BIO GAS ENERGY

PERMANENT